THE CALL
OF THE
LEADER

Michael R. Notaro

For Ish —

All the Best,

Michael Notaro

First published by Dog Ear Publishing
4011 Vincennes Road
Indianapolis, IN 46268
www.dogearpublishing.net

ISBN: 978-145756-684-4

This book is printed on acid-free paper.
Printed in the United States of America

Contents

FOREWORD

I met Michael Notaro early in his leadership journey while speaking at a conference he organized in Berkeley, California, in 2003. He embodied an eagerness to learn, serve, and help others. The Call of the Leader shares the same lucid reasoning and strategic stories that became his trademark serving as president of Toastmasters International in 2011–2012. Whether you are a wannabe leader or seasoned executive, this book is for you. This book will stir you, inspire you, and lift your aspirations in new directions.

Michael has experienced leadership at the top, and he explores why and how he got there. His story is as entertaining as it is educational. There are new concepts and new approaches here that will intrigue and motivate you. He examines the components of what guides a leader into becoming a leader and how the leader can stay close to their source of personal power.

The Call of the Leader helps you reach your full potential and become the leader you are meant to be.

And it is practical. It will help you chart your leadership path if you are not already there, and clear the debris off the path if you are already on it. Then again, if you have arrived at the top already, there's always more room to grow, and Michael will help take you there too. He makes real leadership understandable and accessible to any reader.

The most exciting part of this book is that even those with little or no leadership experience can cultivate greatness through answering *The Call of the Leader.* Yes, *The Call of the Leader* is the fuel that drives the leader. Keep this book close at hand and never let your tank run dry!

Bert Decker
Henderson, Nevada

INTRODUCTION

Are you ready to lead? In a world craving effective leadership, The Call of the Leader takes us back to the source of leadership influence, hearing the voice, recognizing the touch, feeling the emotions, and guiding others with a vision moved by a heartfelt passion for a higher calling. Drawing from lessons learned as 2011–2012 Toastmasters International president, I will show you how to find your unique leadership calling and make a lasting impact. You will learn to embrace leadership not as an obligatory task, but as an authentic expression of your best self.

This book is for those seeking to discover, nurture, and hone their natural leadership skills. Even if you do not think you are a leader, there is one person you lead every single day, and that is *you*!

The call of the leader is the still, small voice that never goes away, aligning your hopes, heart, and head. The call of the leader must live in you before it lives in others; it moves you through aspiration, inspiration, and perspiration. By awakening an authentic, resonant call to leadership, you will forge a unique path to influence. Keep reading and discover the passion, purpose, and power that come from answering *The Call of the Leader*.

Why is this book needed? The need for effective leaders has never been greater. Almost a third of HR executives are struggling to fill senior leadership positions.[1] Fifty-nine percent of companies polled agreed that succession planning is more challenging in today's economy, and nearly half (46 percent) said leadership was the skill hardest to find in employees.[2] Despite the need, public confidence levels in leadership have reached all-time lows. Sixty-nine percent of those polled in the United States say the country has a crisis in leadership.[3] According to the Center for Creative Leadership, between 38 percent and 50 percent of new chief executives fail within their first eighteen months.[4] Most of these leaders are well-educated and technically competent, but there is something missing.

This book is written to change how you fundamentally think about leadership. The world is filled with aspiring leaders who never develop their ability, never attract followers, and never reach their potential. When leaders fail, we all fail. Leadership is more than techniques, tricks, and tactics used to achieve desired results. Only when we access the call of the leader is true leadership potential discovered.

While all leaders face a learning curve, this book will awaken the joy and fun of leadership. *The Call of the Leader* is organized to build your leadership knowledge chapter by chapter. Building on the foundation of personal calling (chapter 1), leadership grows through the expression of passion (chapter 2). Passion is refined by a clear purpose (chapter 3). Purpose focuses energy to generate power (chapter 4). Power emerges from acts of courage (chapter 5). Courage grows through the skillful use of voice (chapter 6). Effective leadership creates a rhythm of success (chapter 7). Successful leaders generate forward momentum by leaving a lasting legacy (chapter 8). Keep reading, and don't quit until you hear your call to leadership.

If you are consumed with busy work—but not your life's work—this book is for you. Will you be my partner in this exciting journey? Applying these principles will change your life and your world. Leadership is a creative art, and the magic is in you. *The Call of the Leader* will stir your spirit, touch your soul, and reveal your potential for greatness … if you let it. Let us begin!

1 CALLING

heard the call of the leader on a hot summer day in August 2007, sitting in a crowded conference room at the Marriot's Desert Ridge Resort in Phoenix, Arizona. I was attending the last day of the Toastmasters International convention, concluding my two-year term on the Toastmasters International board of directors. Happy memories filled my mind. I relished the travel, friendships, and spirited board discussions, which shaped the future of Toastmasters International. But after many years of district and international leadership, I felt my time was over. The transition of power was evident as new, talented leaders emerged. I checked out of the hotel and had my shuttle booked to the airport for my flight back to Oakland, California. Then everything changed.

The closing event of the convention was the Past International Director luncheon. With a grateful heart, I attended in order to chat with new and old friends. Past directors stood and spoke, reflecting on the convention and hopes and dreams for the coming year ahead. The meeting also had a political aspect. At the end, a few past directors stood and announced their intent to run for third vice president of Toastmasters International. This is the officer position that leads directly to Toastmasters International president.

When the luncheon concluded, I gathered my belongings and walked intently toward the exit—my final exit. Just before I reached it, Toastmaster Don Ensch greeted me with a smile and said "Michael, did you announce yourself as a candidate for third vice president?"

"Who me?" I said.

"Yes, are you running for third vice president?"

"Don, I do not think that is for me," I said. "Besides, it would be a lot of work. I have done my time on the board of directors. Running for a big office like that would require an international campaign."

Don looked at me with a long, sympathetic pause. "Young man," he said, "your campaign has already begun!" And he walked away.

At that moment, I felt the call of the leader—a mix of excitement, terror, and anticipation. Don's subtle message was potent and powerful, and the answer calling inside of me was "Yes." But saying yes did not make logical sense at the time. I was planning to step down, not step up. I wanted to fly home, take a break from Toastmasters, and grow my law practice. But Don's words lingered in my heart during the flight home. Somehow, I felt this would not be my last Toastmasters journey.

By the time the plane landed in Oakland, I had mentally prepared to launch my campaign. I quickly announced my candidacy for third vice president, spent a year campaigning, and won election the following year at the Toastmasters International convention in Calgary, Alberta, Canada in 2008. Four years later I served as the 2011–2012 Toastmasters International president.

A calling is defined as "a strong inner impulse toward a particular course of action especially when accompanied by conviction of divine influence."[5] The call of the leader is the decisive force that pulls you toward a daring adventure—a big dream. The voice of opportunity beckons you to fess up, look up, and step up. A larger, richer, and nobler future appears on your landscape. You sense a divine alignment of your talent, spirit, and motivation. A calling may reveal itself through the prodding of others (like my friend Don) or in a moment of quiet reflection (as I felt on the flight home to Oakland). The call of the leader can come in a moment, but it can take a lifetime to find your moment.

The call to leadership is more than a job, task, or activity. It connects *who you are* with *what you are meant to become.* A calling provides a reason to lead. In fact, when you feel the call of the leader, the real question to ask is not "Why?" but "Why not?" The call beckons you to a bigger and better future. It resonates in your heart, mind, and soul; it is your *best* opportunity to add big value to the world. If something fails to move your spirit, it is probably not your calling.

Finding your calling is not something to dread or fear. The call of the leader will expand your vision and impact in the world. Whether you are young or old, discovering your calling is an exciting adventure.

Recognize the Calling

We recognize the call of the leader as an inner voice. While modern life is filled with external voices—bombarding us with demands, expectations, and deadlines—the inner voice is a truer, deeper message. The inner voice comes mainly through feelings, emotions, and thoughts, rather than audible sounds. Our core being communicates moment by moment, providing a wise indicator of inner truth—if we listen. The inner voice is much more than just intuition. Intuition is immediate sensory cognition. A calling lingers much longer, providing an authentic indicator of personal certainty and understanding. Discount your inner voice at your own peril.

But you cannot listen to the inner voice and outer voice at the same time. Listening to the inner voice requires silencing the external voice for a period. Take a break from the muddle of noise and clutter that fills our world. Mindfulness, meditation, and journaling provide helpful internal listening tools. When we shut down the technology (it is possible!) and spend time in silence, focusing on breath, openness, and writing, we experience heightened awareness of thoughts and feelings. If you have never done this, you may experience an aggressive inner critic, a voice of negativity and judgment, trying to disrupt the process. Let the inner critic wind down, and resist the temptation to focus on negative thoughts. Soon, you will feel an internal space emerging. Notice as influential ideas hang around a little longer than others. Like children clamoring for attention, they want your attention. They deserve your attention.

Soon, you will feel the inner voice pulling and tugging at your heartstrings. A calling is the genuine sound resonating within, drawing you toward something bigger than yourself. The ring of authenticity echoes truth within. We find a calling in the heart, not the head. A calling is an exercise of FAITH (Finding Answers in the Heart).

Listen for the hopeful calling, the hard calling, the hidden calling, and the higher calling:

- **Hopeful Calling**: The hopeful calling inspires you to fulfill a heartfelt dream that captivates your spirit. Inspiration powers the calling.

- **Hard Calling**: The hard calling challenges you to develop your full potential when pursuing a difficult challenge. Challenge powers the calling.

- **Hidden Calling**: The hidden calling invites you to pursue the overlooked aspiration of your heart. Fear of loss powers the calling.

- **Higher Calling**: The higher calling stirs you to do noble things that transcend and transform the spirit. Spiritual motives power the calling.

As a grade school student, I was fascinated by the way kids come together and organize themselves. I wanted to see my friends come together and have fun without damaging themselves (the hopeful calling). My favorite subject at school was recess. The energy of my rambunctious classmates playing, laughing, and screaming always made my day. Often, I was called on by adults to maintain order on the playground. Initially, I did not like it much (the hard calling). I felt it ruined my fun, since I liked being the rambunctious one. Over time, however, the peacemaker role started to grow on me (the hidden calling); I realized that if I did not do it, nobody would do it. I felt a transcendent longing to bring diverse groups of kids together (the higher calling).

At that young age, a calling was the furthest thing from my mind, but I knew my peers listened to and respected me. I refereed kickball games, counseled angry kids, and even broke up fights when necessary, keeping the peace despite outbursts from bullies, comics, and cynics. I even came to enjoy eradicating disorder and chaos. Soon, adults asked me to solve behavior problems with kids I had nothing to do with. As I grew older, I kept solving problems for bigger and bigger kids. Today, my law practice solves problems for the biggest kids.

Life presents countless opportunities to discover and develop your calling. Everyone has a calling waiting to be discovered. Notice the times when you feel energized and curious. Ask questions and test assumptions. The merger of facts (objective life experiences) with feelings (intense emotional responses) and faith (conviction of the future) signals a potential calling sweet spot. Here are some notable examples:

1. **Early Calling**: David Copperfield is the most successful magician of my generation, grossing over $4 billion in revenue.[6] By the age of twelve, Copperfield was so consumed with magic that he was invited into the prestigious Society of American Magicians. His calling was unmistakable very early in life.

2. **Mid-life Calling**: Academy-award-winning actor John Houseman (The Paper Chase) was a successful grain speculator in the international grain markets as a young adult. Only after the stock market crash of 1929 did the thirty-one-year-old Houseman try his luck at theater. He found his calling in the middle of his career. Often, an unexpected crisis, divorce, or firing can be the impetus for discovering your calling.

3. **Late Calling**: Harlan Sanders dropped out of school in sixth grade. He worked as a farm hand, mule tender, and service station operator without much success. At sixty-five, Colonel Sanders opened a restaurant, which went bankrupt. Rather than retire, he cashed his first social security check and started the successful Kentucky Fried Chicken (KFC) chain.

Self-awareness and focus will help you recognize your personal calling. When you pursue interests with an open heart and mind, a calling is recognized in the silent spaces between stimulus and response. Reflect on what you could do, might do, and should do. Silent reflection uncovers the depths of motivation rising from oceans of opportunity. Genuine leadership is a public act that springs from a personal longing. The greater your levels of self-awareness, the greater your opportunities for lasting leadership impact.

Early Calling

Jerry Parr was a nine-year-old boy when his father took him to local theater in Miami, Florida.[7] There, Jerry became fascinated by a largely unknown movie called The Code of the Secret Service. The hero of the 1939 Warner Brothers production was a heroic agent named Brass Bancroft, portrayed by an aspiring actor named Ronald Reagan. In the film, Bancroft pursues a ring of Mexican thugs who stole bank plates from the US Treasury. Along the way, Bancroft is blamed for a death, escapes from jail, and finds love. The movie was considered banal, even for the times, and Reagan himself thought it was one of his worst movies.

But young Jerry Parr loved the movie and watched it over and over. He felt the call of the leader. He dreamed of someday becoming a career Secret Service agent. Parr followed his call to leadership; he became a career secret service agent in 1962, the year I was born.

On March 30, 1981, Parr was on duty when President Reagan was shot outside the Washington Hilton. A crazed John W. Hinckley Jr. opened fire on Reagan while the president was exiting after a speech. "When he [Reagan] was about probably six or seven feet from the car, I heard these shots," Parr said. "I sort of knew what they were, and I'd been waiting for them my entire career, in a way. That's what every agent waits for, is that."[8]

Parr got hold of Reagan, pushed him into the presidential limousine, and then jumped in on top of him. Parr shouted to the driver, "Take off!" When Reagan started spitting up blood, Parr made the split-second decision to divert the president's limousine to the emergency room of George Washington University Medical Center. The decision may have saved Reagan's life; he underwent two hours of surgery to remove a .22-caliber bullet, then returned to the White House twelve days later.

Jerry Parr is the Secret Service agent credited with saving President Reagan's life. "It was such a strange thing," Mr. Parr said, "seeing his image on a film when I was 9 years old, and then I ended up helping save his life."[9]

Reagan believed God saved him for a new season of public service. He referred to the borrowed time, which extended his call to leadership. The little-known movie *The Code of the Secret Service*—which Reagan thought was unimportant work—was actually a life-saving work. It inspired Jerry Parr to recognize his life calling, which in turn saved Reagan's life forty-two years later. Interestingly, Parr also believed that

God had directed his life path to save Reagan. After retiring from the Secret Service in 1985, he became a pastor.

Like Reagan, we all have seemingly insignificant events in life that are crucial to our growth and development. Sometimes, those events are crucial to our survival. Our callings intersect with others to reveal and guide deeper truths. Even a terrible tragedy can provide the fertile ground for the discovery of a fresh calling. Listen for the call of your heart. The sooner you recognize it, the better.

Divine Calling

Are you attuned to your calling? A calling is revealed in a myriad of different shapes and forms—in times of good and bad, abundance and scarcity, happiness and sadness. It can also come when you least expect it, disrupting and even reversing your life path. For example, Saul of Tarsus built a reputation threatening and tormenting Christians. One day while traveling on a Damascus road, he was struck by a blinding light from Heaven (Acts 9:3, NIV). He fell to the ground and heard a voice say to him, "Saul, Saul, why do you persecute me?"

"Who are you, Lord?" Saul asked.

"I am Jesus, whom you are persecuting," he replied. "Now get up and go into the city, and you will be told what you must do."

Speechless and blind, Paul was led to Damascus, where a disciple named Ananias gave further direction. Ananias placed his hands on Saul, restored his sight, lifted his spirit, and affirmed his calling to proclaim the Christian gospel to the Gentiles. The calling was from God, but the vision came through people.

Saul's calling transformed him from a zealous persecutor of the Christian faith to its most ardent proponent. This uniquely talented leader emerged and followed his life calling. Today, his inspired writings consume much of the New Testament. Paul's personal transformation illustrates the power of a divine voice calling a person to leadership. The call of Saul of Tarsus was unmistakable; he could not have missed it if he'd tried. God knew that Paul was so committed to persecuting Christians that it would take something dramatic to get his attention.

Paul's transformation illustrates the three P's of a leadership calling. The calling must be possible, personal, and practical:

- **A Possible Calling**: Paul's call infused him with the possible. The nascent Christian Church was struggling but had tremendous growth potential under the right leadership. He knew the Church could grow only when the individual members were growing personally. He also knew achieving the possible required him to give up the comforts of Roman citizenry for the hardship of becoming a traveling disciple who was beaten, maligned, imprisoned, and shipwrecked. Achieving the possible required personal sacrifice.

- **A Personal Calling**: God called Paul by name with a personal call to leadership. Paul was particularly well-suited to leadership because his background bridged civic influence and spirituality. He was a Roman citizen, with all its rights and privileges. At the same time, he had been born to Jewish parents and given strict training in the law. From age ten to fifteen, he studied the Hebrew scriptures in the city of Jerusalem under Rabbi Gamaliel.[10] Paul leveraged his unique training to evangelize the diverse Gentile population and grow the early church.

- **A Practical Calling**: Paul was gifted with the practical skills of leadership. He was a clear and cogent thinker with a penetrating speaking style. He spoke in a plain, straightforward way that deviated from the flowery oratory of the day. He spoke to both the common man and the well-educated, with a practical message of personal renewal and life change.

A calling is an invitation that beckons you by name for a mission uniquely suited to your gifts and abilities. Like a custom-fitted suit, your calling is designed for nobody but you. Your calling may live in the voice of an expectant child, a supportive friend, or a demanding spouse. Your calling may spring from open opportunities caused by an unexpected job termination. Your calling may live in a partnership that brings you joy and life meaning. A calling is the symphony of influence that cannot be silenced. Are you listening?

Paul's call to leadership contrasts starkly with another biblical character: the prophet Elijah, who experienced a divine calling in a much quieter way that made him stop and listen closely. Elijah was called to oppose a wicked king and bring revival to his people. Like many of us, Elijah's life was an emotional rollercoaster. At times he was bold, expectant, and confident. At other times, he was lonely, discouraged, and fearful. He slipped into depression when Ahab's wife, Jezebel, vowed to kill him. Anxious Elijah was deeply absorbed in the stress and tumult of his life problems. He desired a dramatic divine intervention to inspire and lift him, but he was sadly mistaken. Standing atop a mountain, Elijah learned that his calling came not in an earthquake, not in wind, and not in fire, but in the still, small voice (1 Kings 19:11).

The still, small voice is literally the sound of soft stillness. When Elijah slowed, stopped, and waited for the silent, inaudible voice, he found his divine calling. God's voice was heard, and Elijah went on to be taken up to Heaven in a whirlwind (2 Kings 2:1–11).

While the calling of Saul was overwhelming and dramatic, the calling of Elijah was quiet and soft. The call to leadership is different for each of us. Each of us has different gifts and talents. We each have rich life experiences that can be used to make us more effective leaders. One thing is certain: The call to leadership is the invitation to an uncommon life. Life is filled with callings. Some are large; some are small. Some are ignored; some are acted upon. Personal fulfillment is closely tied to recognizing and responding to your calling.

Receive the Calling

The call of the leader is a respected voice that cuts through the avalanche of information and technology. It is the voice that beckons you to follow your dreams, take a risk, and make an impact. Receiving the call to leadership is like standing in a crowded ballroom with too many people. The conversations grow steadily louder as hundreds strain to be heard. Soon, the wall of sound is deafening; you can barely hear the person three feet in front of you. Suddenly, from the other side of the room, you miraculously hear your name spoken. The world stops. External noises are tuned out. You immediately swing your full attention to the sound of your name. Like a distant cry, the call of the leader calls for you and you alone.

The most important voice is the silent one within. Are you listening for the hopeful voice, the hard voice, the hidden voice, or the higher voice? Are you listening to the pesky agitator, the curious observer, or the treasured friend? The call of the leader requires openness to the organic forces shaping your life.

Listening to the inner voice is difficult in a world of constant distractions. From texting to tweeting, media hype to media gripe, technology keeps us reacting and responding. The superficial deluge is overwhelming. Many silence the inner voice to their own detriment. Imagine if young Jerry Parr had been too busy playing video games to see *The Code of the Secret Service*. Imagine if Saint Paul had been too busy listening to iTunes to recognize the blinding light from Heaven. Both would have missed their calling!

Responding to the Calling

A calling is a verb; it requires responsive action. If you are not moved to act, you have not found your calling. Imagine someone you love calling your name—an appeal from a suffering child or friend in pain. Would you waste time? Would you take the attitude "Don't bother me because I'm busy"? I hope not. When you know the voice calling and you know it is calling for you, the response is immediate and swift. A sincere call prompts heartfelt action.

"Successful people keep moving," said Conrad Hilton.[11] As you seek out your calling, explore natural curiosities and interests. Pursue new horizons and uncharted paths. Action gets you moving in the direction of your calling. Chart your growth with baby steps, bright steps, and bold steps:

- **Baby Steps**: Dr. Martin Luther King Jr. said, "Take the first step in faith. You don't have to see the whole staircase, just take the first step."[12] Aspiring leaders start with small steps. My Toastmasters journey began with one tiny speech at UC Berkeley. Start your engine and begin inching forward even if you do not have all the answers. Try something new that pushes you outside of your comfort zone. At the least, you will learn something that is *not* your calling. Small, reliable steps provide experience and leadership momentum.

- **Bright Steps**: Take a bright step by investing in personal growth and development. When I graduated from law school, jobs were scarce, so I took an uncommon step—I volunteered to work at a successful law practice for free in return for the experience. Later, as my practice grew, I paid top-flight attorneys for their valuable practice insights. Bright steps increase your knowledge and experience. Leaders go the extra mile to hone their skills and acquire helpful information. Find a mentor to help you develop your leadership skills and reap a rich bounty.

- **Bold Steps**: "Freedom lies in being bold," said Robert Front.[13] Leaders who chase a hard calling or hidden calling require a daring spirit. Never be afraid to take a risk; never be afraid to move from the safe zone to the faith zone. Leaders are not afraid to take a misstep or overstep. They take strategic risks when necessary and avoid overthinking decisions, which brings the slow death of paralysis by analysis. The apostle Paul took a bold step when a higher calling changed his life focus from hate to love. Bold steps challenge us to sell out for our calling.

Responding to the call of the leader is a lifelong process. It reminds me of the call and response of a Southern preacher delivering a sermon. The familiar invitation "Can I get an amen?" always finds a responsive "Amen!" The back-and-forth between the preacher and congregation creates a rhythm of connection and collaboration. Similarly, your leadership growth involves a call and response with your deepest motivations and longings. The collaboration with your inner voice shapes your public leadership. Remember, you do not find your leadership calling; it finds you. That discovery comes through a lifetime of testing, tuning, and trusting skills:

- **Test Your Skills**: Your life call-in is really a call-out to test and grow your professional skills. Testing skills brings self-awareness through practice and experiential learning. As you cultivate communication, strategic-planning, team-building, and problem-solving skills, the hopeful calling becomes a possible and even probable calling. A calling is the goal, but skill development is the means to take you there. In general, those with limited skills have low leadership potential. In fact, a leader without skills is like a car without gas—you go nowhere. In contrast, those who develop versatile skills have strong leadership potential. Test your calling, grow your skills, and expand your leadership potential.

- **Tune Your Skills**: Leaders tune their personal skills, growing from incompetence to competence and mastery. They refine the skills necessary for their chosen industry and usually achieve excellence in at least one crucial skill area. It may be public speaking, emotional intelligence, or decision-making. Tune in to the call and response between human emotions and aspirations to motivate followers. Be willing to self-correct, admit your failures, and learn from every mistake, which will make you a transparent, credible leader.

- **Trust Your Skills**: "He who does not trust enough, will not be trusted," said Lao Tzu.[14] Trust is a relational dynamic that must be earned and can never be forced. Trust is really authenticity, being true to your calling and true to the vision you create for others. You will never convince others to trust you unless you trust yourself. Leaders who test and tune their skills build a strong foundation for positive trust. I once gave a speech before a voting assembly of thousands and faced an aggressive heckler in the audience. I trusted my speaking skills built from decades of practice to persevere through adversity. When we trust ourselves, we allow others to trust in themselves, and our leadership can flourish.

One of the best ways to test, tune, and trust your skills is through nonprofit service organizations. Unlike paid employment, nonprofit work is gratis service. Organic leadership grows through relational influence. In fact, some of the world's most successful leaders developed their skills through nonprofit service. US president John F. Kennedy, Supreme Court justice Samuel Alito, and former Green Bay Packers coach Vince Lombardi were all active in the Knights of Columbus. Seven past US presidents (Teddy Roosevelt, Harding, Franklin Roosevelt, Truman, Kennedy, Carter, and Reagan), along with Jimmy Durante, Bob Hope, and Arnold Palmer were all members of the Fraternal Order of Eagles, and past first ladies Eleanor Roosevelt and Bess Truman were members of the Ladies Auxiliary. Famous Rotarians include Colonel Sanders, Winston Churchill, and Sam Walton. Notable Toastmasters include Debbi Rose Fields (founder of Mrs. Fields Bakeries), Peter Coors of Coors Brewery, former Hawaii governor Linda Lingle, and former US speaker of the house Carl Albert. Yes, service organizations nurture the call of the leader.

Life is filled with opportunities for leadership. Some are large; some are small. Some are ignored; some are acted upon. Some may exist for a season and later dissipate or disappear. The call of the leader is a path slowly illuminated through personal action, which reveals a joyful, vibrant, and exciting life.

Perhaps nothing about leadership particularly excites you. If you feel no call to leadership now, continue pursuing your passions, testing your interests, and tuning your skills. Focus your life on exemplary service and adding value to others. Over time, your life patterns and habits will reveal predicable clues to your calling. When you least expect it, an event will trigger recognition of your calling, and when it appears, you will wonder why it took so long to recognize it.

This book will help you build awareness of your calling. You will learn to recognize leadership opportunities, tune into your better self, and align your natural talents to seize the moment when it arrives. Followers are drawn not just by what you say but by what you become.

Summary

The call of the leader makes you the steward of something bigger than yourself. In the ancient world, a steward was entrusted with managing, protecting, and enriching the property of their master. The steward had to be trustworthy and accountable, or they didn't last very long. As leaders, we are stewards of the calling to which we are entrusted. We are caretakers for a larger vision, a bigger purpose, and a greater calling.

The call of the leader is an opportunity waiting to be discovered and seized. It may appear as a hope, dream, or aspiration that calls, beckons, and invites. It may raise its head in times of adversity or success. Others may notice your natural propensities and comment that you should do other things with your life. But only you can recognize and release your authentic leadership calling—not your kids, spouse, parents, or boss. It is for you and you alone.

You can avoid or ignore your calling, but you can never silence the urge to live your dreams. Inside each of us, there is a hopeful calling, a hard calling, a hidden calling, and a higher calling. The discovery may come early or late in life; your calling is personal, possible, and practical. Take action on your calling. The baby steps will grow into bold steps as confidence and self-assurance increases. Seize the moment to test, tune, and trust your skills.

To get the full benefit of this book, you must apply the principles you learn. Leadership is experiential learning. We grow through trial and error, success and failure. When reflection complements experience, the seeds of leadership greatness are planted. Robert Allen said, "Everything you want is just outside your comfort zone."[15] Are you ready to experience your leadership accelerator? Do you have the courage to take your foot off the brake? Divine power is released when you let go of your inhibitions and let greatness flow. Man's extremity is divine opportunity. Isn't it time to stop shrinking in insecurity and start claiming the abundant bounty you deserve?

2 PASSION

Passion is the fire within your spirit. Merriam-Webster's Online Dictionary defines passion as "an intense, driving or overmastering feeling or conviction."[16] Passion ignites action and gets you moving in life. A leader with passion radiates energy and boundless opportunity. If you lack passion, your leadership is defeated before it starts.

Calling reveals passion. It is not enough to feel led in a certain direction. Leaders learn to uncover the passion that engages the head, embraces the heart, and inspires the spirit. Picture multiple tributaries flowing into a mighty river. Each tributary represents the interests of a solitary leader. Passion is the downstream force that pulls multiple tributaries into a powerful river. Passion is the heartbeat calling us to unite, energize, and advance together.

Many have spent a lifetime denying their passions. To conform to the expectations of others, passions are denied and dreams are ignored. Pursuing a safe, predictable career path may put food on the table and pay the bills, but the call of the leader never settles for conformity and mediocrity.

Finding your passion is the first step to living your passion. As leaders express deeper emotions, they inevitably draw the attention and curiosity of others. When passion and calling align, a roaring river of opportunity emerges. The powerful current is often turbulent and choppy. The key skill is learning to direct your passion in a healthy, productive way that multiplies followers. The infectious, contagious passion of a leader will always attract followers. This chapter will not only help you identify your passion but also help you refine your passion for maximum leadership impact. Without passion, leadership is drudgery. With passion, leadership is exhilarating. Keep reading and discover the power of passion.

The Passion Difference

While I was in my twenties, I served on the board of directors for an important community service organization. The president of the board was a docile, low-energy man. I will call him Henry. Henry spoke with a monotone, reading board minutes and reports word for word. He rarely made eye contact with others. Henry was a human sleeping pill, and his meetings were painful to endure. With Henry at the helm, I was so bored with the board that I dreamed of getting to the exit as quickly as possible.

A few years later, I served on a different leadership committee with a leader I will call Clyde. Clyde exuded passion and excitement. He smiled, laughed, and engaged team members with eye contact and vocal variety. He listened and made me feel understood, appreciated, and empowered. He united others with his overwhelming passion and excitement for the great things we could do working together. His drive was more than a goal or objective; it was a mission, and it showed. He wanted to produce the best results possible and had clear expectations for our precious time together. Which leader—Henry or Clyde—do you think was more effective? For me, the answer is obvious: It was Clyde.

Henry taught me how fatigue dooms leadership, but Clyde taught me how passion overcomes fatigue. Leadership without passion is dead on arrival, while leadership powered by genuine passion is virtually unstoppable. Passion links your calling with your leadership style and purpose. Every day is a celebration of the mission. Small victories become big victories, and big victories become movement milestones. The leader's passion for a new product, service, or method rallies others to the cause.

Passion is learning your calling, loving your calling, and living your calling. What are the keys to becoming a passionate leader? There are three essential steps, which I call the three Es: energy, enthusiasm, and engagement.

- **Energy**: Leaders need high levels of energy. Without energy, your leadership car runs out of gas. When the energy vibrations increase, hope rises. You maintain energy by staying in your sweet spot, doing the things you love, and releasing other vital tasks to others. Energy requires maintaining margin in your life. Go for a walk, meditate, listen to inspirational music, journal. Energy is created in the open spaces of life. If you have no open spaces, you energy will deplete, and your leadership will suffer.

- **Enthusiasm**: Enthusiasm is zeal and fervor rising from genuine excitement. An enthusiastic leader has the winning edge in life. It begins on the inside: The last four letters of enthusiasm are IASM, which stands for "I Am Sold, Myself." When the leader truly believes in their cause, they become an unstoppable force. You must sell yourself before selling others. How do you activate group enthusiasm? Ask one simple question: "What is the best thing that can happen while we are together?" Then act as if the best thing will happen.

- **Engagement**: Engagement mobilizes human energy to pull people together, creating a unified, caring community. The leader connects team members to something bigger than themselves. Engagement is a byproduct of the love people feel for each other and connection to their cause.

Energy, enthusiasm, and engagement all require vitality. Vitality is derived from the Latin word for "vital force or life."[17] Vitality is the exuberant physical strength that we feel and radiate to others. To maintain vitality, we need to maintain health and strength. This requires regular exercise, eating healthy foods, and avoiding harmful activities. As president of Toastmasters, I often found myself at evening events surrounded by members who did not want me to leave. I had a policy of not drinking alcohol, not overeating, and going to my room by 10:00 p.m. Some criticized me for ruining the fun, but I was focusing on maintaining vitality for the next day.

Find Your Leadership Passion

Finding your leadership passion is finding your big joy. Where do you find your big joy? By journaling, meditation, and digging deeply into life experiences, we find a natural source of percolating passion and energy. Personal introspection reveals a bountiful treasure within, and big joy lives at the passionate ends of your extremities. Engage a trusted friend or advisor who knows you well to assist. Here are a few issues to consider:

1. **Inspiration**: What inspires you to take action? Inspire comes from the Latin word inspirare, which means literally "blow into or breathe upon."[18] All of us have something inside that moves us to take action in the world. Notice the breath of personal motivation that gets you out of bed each morning.

2. **Talent**: What activities come easiest to you? We all have natural talents, gifts, and abilities. I like to teach, coach, and train, and they come easily to me. Exploration brings revelation. You might be a natural artist, entrepreneur, athlete, writer, or speaker. Of course, it takes work to develop your calling, but finding your natural source of joy, not suffering, is a great place to start.

3. **Value**: Where do you provide the most value to others? Notice when you do something that makes others happy, wealthy, or successful. Conversely, notice when your best efforts still leave others feeling dry and empty. Take note of subtle compliments like "You seem to be really good at this."

4. **Experience**: What problems are you uniquely suited to solve? Your education and experience uniquely position you to do things others cannot. Leverage the best of your background to create a sweet spot that merges experience and passion. What is your sweet spot?

5. **Meaning**: What gives you meaning and fulfillment? Joy and pleasure are byproducts of following a fulfilling life calling. Do you remember your first love? Return to the early activities that brought you joy and satisfaction.

Spend time with people who ignite your passions and your passion will become contagious.

A Passion for Numbers

Born in 1937, Charles grew up in Woodland, California—a small farm community west of Sacramento. The family used ration stamps to buy food during World War II. Young Charles worked on the farm, bagging walnuts and selling eggs door-to-door. He found a way to make extra money after high school football games by collecting discarded Coca-Cola bottles, which he cashed in for pennies per bottle. As an Avon boy, he rode around the neighborhood, delivering cosmetic products. He pushed an ice cream cart during the summer and even sold chicken droppings as fertilizer.

Charles graduated from Santa Barbara High School in 1959 as captain of the golf team and found acceptance at Stanford University. His first year was a disaster; he failed both English and French. He later learned he was dyslexic; basic reading and writing were traumatic events. To get through school, he relied on comic book reading and sympathetic friends to help with writing papers and notes. While his writing skills were limited, Charles always excelled in quantitative and technical subjects. A persistent but handicapped student, Charles graduated from Stanford in 1959 with a BA degree in economics and an MBA in 1961.

In 1963, Charles and three partners launched a successful investment newsletter; he later started one of the country's first no-load mutual funds. But a crushing, unexpected lawsuit from regulators brought everything to a screeching halt. By 1972, his company and mutual fund were in tatters, and his reputation was destroyed. Life hit a low point; he was $100,000 in debt, and his wife filed for divorce. Searching for new direction in life, he enrolled in law school, hoping to emulate his father and grandfather, who were both lawyers. But after just three weeks, he was overwhelmed by the required reading and writing, so he quit.

Charles had a driving personal and professional passion; he wanted to level the playing field for the common man investing in stocks. He said, "I have a passion for the investor. I've always been one myself ..."[19] Charles believed uppity stock brokers exploited the public, charging excessive commission fees. He described Wall Street financiers as a den of thieves who aggressively sold risky securities and made exorbitant profits while consumers suffered. He wanted it to change. He had a passion for bringing financial independence to the common man.

A turning point came in 1975 when the US Securities and Exchange Commission deregulated the securities industry. His passion and calling meshed as he seized the opportunity to start Charles Schwab and Company, a discount brokerage company. His mission was simple: to help ordinary people achieve financial independence by providing discount brokerage services. His calling aligned intensive research and the dogged persistence of a dyslexic student to empower the consumer. By the time Schwab retired in 2008, his company had become the largest discount security dealer in the United States, helping millions achieve financial independence.[20]

A Passion for People

Passionate leaders leave a lasting impression by positively transforming the lives of others. For me, there was one who did it the best. His name was Cavett Robert, the only person in Toastmasters International history to win both the World Championship of Public Speaking (1942) and the

Golden Gavel Award (1972). I met Cavett when we shared a meal at the Toastmasters International convention in Palm Desert, California, in 1989. I was twenty-seven years old, and he was eighty-one—and an accomplished salesman, public speaker, and real estate lawyer. Cavett took an interest in me, which I reciprocated. He sent me free cassette tapes on how to be a better speaker and leader. Over time, I found my life mirroring my Toastmasters mentor. Cavett was a salesman; I was a salesman. Cavett was a public speaker; I was a public speaker. Cavett was realtor; I was a realtor. Cavett was a real estate lawyer; I was a real estate lawyer.

Cavett's life was a source of inspiration. Born in Starkville, Mississippi, in 1907, he graduated from Ole Miss in 1929 and began teaching in a one-room schoolhouse in Prairie Point, Mississippi. He then worked as a gas-line installer before attending Washington and Lee University School of Law. He went on to practice law in Virginia, New York, and Arizona, and even served as a judge. Cavett became an accomplished salesman, selling everything from insurance to cemetery plots. Arizona Edison Power Company hired him to visit small towns, where he spoke to Toastmasters, churches, and service clubs. Although it is hard to believe, Cavett acknowledged suffering from extreme stage fright in his early years. He overcame his fears to become an accomplished and highly sought-after professional speaker on sales and motivational topics. Cavett leveraged his Toastmasters training to found the National Speakers Association, the preeminent trade organization for professional speakers with thousands of members.

Cavett gave his first paid speech when he was sixty-one years of age! When most people think about retirement, Cavett chose *refirement*: He launched a twenty-five-year career as a professional speaker. If only he had discovered his speaking talent earlier in life! As a late bloomer, he brought to the speaking professional rich lessons from his personal experiences. Cavett had a unique ability to bring people together with his charm, wisdom, and encouragement. He was a speaker's speaker, and his spirit and generosity continues to motivate speakers around the world.

I was grateful and a bit surprised that a man of his stature would give me so much attention without compensation. It felt like I won the inspiration lottery. Cavett passed away in 1997, but his book *Success with People* remains a classic on my nightstand. I read it over and over again. His life embodied a powerful message of achievement from humble roots.

For years I wondered how Cavett, a bubbling fountain of enthusiasm, maintained his passion for life and leadership. Did he ever sleep? His demonstrative style kept expectant audiences waiting on every word. His interests were diverse and varied. Initially, I thought his passions were sales, real estate, and leadership, but I soon realized that those things were merely expressions of his deeper passion. His real passion was people. "A desire to help others is our most noble attribute; it gives immortal momentum to life and is our only certain path to heaven," said Cavett.[21] He loved people, and sales, public speaking, and leadership were his chosen vehicles for service. Love was the spiritual glue that held his life together. In recognition of Cavett, the National Speakers Association annually bestows its highest award, the Cavett Award, to honor members whose careers demonstrate the spirit of sharing, guiding, and inspiring other professional speakers.

I learned three "Be" principles of "being" from Cavett:

- **Be Authentic**: Cavett believed in finding the truth, speaking the truth, and living the truth. Each speech communicated his authentic passion for serving others. He was a master salesman but never sold or pitched his ideas. Rather, he listened and shared the best solution to each need. He said, "You can persuade more people by the depths of your conviction than the heights of your logic."[22]

- **Be Inclusive**: Cavett believed in working through people rather than doing things to people. He touched ever-expanding audiences with his positive ideas for personal development. When he spoke, every person in the audience felt included and appreciated. His homespun stories and illustrations helped others recognize and develop their natural talent and ability.

- **Be Positive**: Cavett once told an audience "I would rather be around a man who steals my money than a man who steals my optimism." His positive mental attitude was contagious. His exuberance for life and service to others was unquenchable. More than a Pollyanna approach, he taught people to believe in themselves and take action with resolve to serve others.

Refresh Your Passion

Leaders develop a system to refresh, renew, and recharge their batteries. The trials and stress of leadership can drag you down and diminish your passion. It may require a sabbatical, mini-break, or diminishing work. Leaders who become enmeshed in the details or micromanaging get exhausted fast. A little rest will help you pull back and get perspective. Rest gives the clarity and energy needed to persevere.

Burned-out leaders manifest PDS: Passion Deficiency Syndrome. How do you recognize PDS? You have a constant feeling of exhaustion, anxiety, and restlessness. Hating your work reveals PDS. Turning to drugs or alcohol to cope reveals PDS. The leader without passion is pulling dead weight. Followers do not want to invest their time and energy in a leader who lacks passion, which is often interpreted to mean lacking conviction. The passion of the leader must be more intense than the followers.

I have had PDS in my life, and I bet you have too. Over half of all US workers report that they are dissatisfied at times with their jobs.[23] Many never feel engaged or connected to their work. The burdens and obligations of life often pull us away from our true passions. We feel a constant pressure to pay the mortgage, care for the children, and conform to the expectations of others. As children, we obey our parents or face discipline. At school, we obey our teachers or face expulsion. At college, we obey our professors or face failure. At work, we obey our employer or get fired. Soon, life is over, and we hardly recognize our passions. "Many people die with their music still in them. Too often it is because they are always getting ready to live. Before they know it time runs out," said Oliver Wendell Holmes Sr.[24]

I am not suggesting that you throw in the towel with every discouragement. Leadership is filled with difficult and taxing times. No leader experiences eternal bliss and constant adoration. Failure and frustration is part of leadership, and feelings will come and go like a fickle lover. Physical health and self-care may shape your feelings. Lack of support may change your feelings. Leadership passion is bigger than individual feelings. The ebb and flow of emotion is natural. Passion is the flow that keeps you making the difference that changes the world. When we get too comfortable and stop taking risks, we lose our passion.

Authors Robert Kriegel and Louis Patler cite a study of 1,500 young people embarking upon their career.[25] The group was divided into two groups based on their primary work motivation: 83 percent chose their career based on money-making potential, and 17 percent chose their career based on love for the work (passion) with little concern for money. At the end of twenty years, 101 had become millionaires, and all but one of the millionaires was from the group who had chosen their career based on passion.

Called leaders have bigger motivations than just money, titles, or external accolades. They want to make a difference in life. They want to make the world a better place, enhance potential, and end human suffering. For me, living with passion is mental health. I have had high-paying jobs that bring no personal satisfaction. Life is short, and working in a dreary job in a dreary environment makes life shorter and depressing. Negative things will fill the vacuum and zap our energy. Learning to express convictions and desires are natural if you feel passionate. If you are not passionate, you cannot steal enthusiasm if you try. The best way to burn out is to accept a job for high pay where you feel no passion.

Discovering your passion can be easy and obvious or excruciatingly difficult. When you hit rock bottom, it is often found. Sometimes, there is a life turning point that brings you to your senses—a dying child, a major car accident, being fired from a secure job, etc. Often, discovering your passion requires letting go of the safe and secure to move out of your comfort zone.

Many discover or rediscover their life passion at midlife after a misfortune, accident, burnout, or growth experience. When the weight of life makes you feel weak and constricted, it is time to slow down. The pressure to conform to the expectations of others in our culture is overwhelming. At some point, a leader must grow their individual passion into a collective group passion. Otherwise, a leader does everything alone. Passionate leaders must have faith in others. They look for others to engage in their passion.

I graduated from the University of California, Berkeley, in 1985. After several corporate interviews, I realized I was not cut out for the traditional corporate career. Pushing papers and climbing the corporate ladder was not for me. I kept looking and looking and looking. I had a few job offers, but nothing felt right.

Then a position appeared that seemed to have my name on it. It was an entry-level research position at a commercial real estate company. There was one problem, however: My starting salary was the minimum wage of $3.35 an hour, less FICA withholding. Of course, I knew I would work more than forty hours a week, but the company made it clear I would only be paid for forty hours.

Friends thought I was crazy for accepting such a low salary. It was embarrassing to gather with my college graduate friends and discuss salary. Not only was I the lowest-paid by a long shot, but they reminded me that I was paid less than the janitor. Still, it never bothered me. In my view, following my passion was the opportunity of a lifetime, regardless of the low pay. It was my chance to break into an interesting and dynamic field, and I have never regretted following my calling instead of choosing the highest-paid entry-level position.

From Passion to Compassion

Many find their passion in feeling compassion for others. Regardless of our background, all of us will experience pain, tragedy, and suffering in life. Without it, we are not human. Some experience more misfortune than others. Compassion is a word derived from the Latin root cum, which means with, and passio, which means to feel suffering. Compassion is literally suffering with others; it is that deep awareness of another's sorrow, anguish, and distress that moves the leader to respond. The call of the leader is often motivated by compassion for suffering more than zeal for triumph.

Compassion moved Dr. Martin Luther King Jr. to care for the plight of fellow African-Americans and work to create a world where people are judged not by the color of their skin but the conduct of their character. His work in founding the Southern Christian Leadership Conference (SCLC) in 1957—in which he was active until his death—mobilized black churches to protest the injustice of racial segregation. Compassion deepened Dr. King's moral authority and drive to succeed. Compassion moves the call of the leader. Opportunities for compassionate leadership are limitless. While every profession needs compassionate leaders, every leader is not compassionate.

Compassion emerged in my life one fateful day: October 17, 1989. It started just like an ordinary workday for me, but it did not end that way. As a busy commercial real estate broker, I planned a building tour in West Oakland with a company president considering relocation. At the last minute, my client called and cancelled the building tour. He planned to go home early and watch the third game of the World Series between the San Francisco Giants and Oakland Athletics. I gladly accepted his request because I also wanted to get home early and watch the game. Before leaving the office, I gathered my papers and closed my desk. Suddenly, a violent 6.9-magnitude earthquake shook my thirteenth-floor office in downtown Oakland. The floor began to shake and quiver; I was thrown from side to side. My coworkers seemed to dance uncontrollably as everyone searched for stable footing, and I searched for a stairway to get out.

Although the earthquake only lasted from ten to fifteen seconds, the damage was devastating. The quake killed sixty-three people throughout Northern California. It injured 3,757 and left many thousands homeless. Most of the fatalities occurred just blocks from my office, when a two-level freeway overpass, the Cypress Street Viaduct, collapsed, and forty-one people died instantly. The elevated Cypress Freeway had been built on filled marshland; during the quake, it buckled and collapsed, with the upper deck crashing down on scores of ensnared cars that had been traveling on the lower deck. On the upper deck, cars were thrown and flipped, with some left dangling on the edge of the highway. A friend from my church was one of the fatalities.

Amidst the rumble and wreckage, ordinary people heard the call to leadership and stepped up to help. Bystanders, workers, and neighbors climbed amidst the rubble that was the Cypress Freeway and worked tirelessly to extract wounded and trapped people from disfigured cars, offering assistance and hope until emergency crews arrived. Local factory workers drove heavy lifting equipment to the scene and started raising sections of the fallen freeway, hoping to rescue the people underneath. Neighbors bound together to offer meals, respite, and spiritual support.

The magnitude of the loss and its unexplainable nature left many feeling empty and searching for answers. Grieving spread throughout the Oakland community; the numbing pain of human loss slowly shifted to malaise and despair. But leaders rallied from all points to support the community in our time of despair. One of them was Toastmasters International president John Noonan from British Colombia, Canada, who refused to cancel his planned visit to the area. His inspirational words shared at the District 57 Toastmasters Convention in November 1989 provided hope to me and countless others. The Quake of 1989 left a devastating scar but also berthed grassroots leadership in the Oakland community. People who had neglected the depressed West Oakland neighborhood suddenly took note and thought of ways to help the community. I found myself more involved in West Oakland, giving, serving and helping those in need. While the electrical lights went out for 1.4 million people, the spiritual light of compassion never dimmed. I transformed from self-focus to other-focus. I gave my time, money, and attention to helping friends and family of those lost in the tragedy.

As leaders, we can build bridges of compassion when suffering is greatest. Looters and opportunists exploit tragedy; leaders use tragedy to mobilize the best parts of their character. Compassionate leadership changes the mood and helps people recognize the lost beauty within. When we fully release the sorrow, we can fully embrace the joy. A leader fueled by compassion breaks negative strongholds to transform and elevate others.

Summary

Passion is the rocket fuel of leadership. Without it, leaders stumble through life stale and anemic.

How do you find passion? Passion is learning your calling, loving your calling, and living your calling. Release passion through finding your source of energy, enthusiasm, and engagement with others. Notice the special moments in life that inspire you, reveal your talent, show your value, leverage your experience, or create special meaning.

Leadership requires a passion for people. Toastmaster Cavett Robert taught three principles of "Be": be authentic, be inclusive, and be positive. Leadership is hard work. At times, we all need time to refresh, renew, and recharge our batteries. But if your work constantly feels exhausting and futile, perhaps you have Passion Deficiency Syndrome (PDS). Passion bypass surgery can change your life flow to reveal an authentic life calling.

Finding your life calling is as much about compassion as passion. What do you care deeply about? Do you identify with the sorrow, anguish, and distress of others? The call of the leader is often motivated more by compassion for others than passion for self. Tragedy reveals opportunity for leaders willing to seize the challenge. Passion launches your leadership journey, but the subject of our next chapter (purpose) is necessary for progress. Keep reading!

3 PURPOSE

W hat is your leadership purpose? Purpose is a reason you act. The call of the leader reveals a hard-wired purpose, which propels forward progress. Leaders refine purpose into a specific resolve, an enduring intention, which releases powerful natural energy. Purpose is the rudder that steers the leadership ship.

I once toured the command bridge of the USS *Enterprise*, the world's first nuclear-powered aircraft carrier, and watched a young navy helmsmen steer the 94,781-metric-ton ship through San Francisco Bay. "Big E" (as the carrier was known) was once home to over 5,800 sailors. The helmsmen carefully charted a safe course of passage for the enormous vessel.

Steering a ship of this magnitude is no easy task, requiring many years of training and experience. The helmsmen must steer the rudder while compensating for changing sea conditions like rough seas, strong winds, or powerful swells. Similarly, each leader needs a resolute purpose to guide them through the storms of life to reach a desired destination. While you may feel tempted to panic, learn to maintain a cool head, a calm heart, and a clear focus. A clear purpose will quiet your nerves and inspire those around you.

Life is the precious cargo you steer every single day through turbulent waters. You may steer to a beautiful shore or crash into the rocks. The choice is yours. Make time to guide your important voyage with a clear personal purpose. "In our work training thousands of managers at organizations from GE to the Girl Scouts, and teaching an equal number of executives and students at Harvard Business School, we've found that fewer than 20% of leaders have a strong sense of their own individual purpose," wrote Nick Craig and Scott A. Snook in a May 2014 article titled "From Purpose to Impact."[26] Leadership can be confounding and confusing. This chapter will show you how to forge a clear leadership purpose that moves you forward toward fulfilling your calling.

Seek a Purpose

Purpose is a tool of full engagement, directing the clearest path for your leadership journey. Many well-intentioned leaders think they must confine themselves to one rigid path to success. Not so. This is the reason so many leaders feel empty and adrift, like something is missing. The helmsmen must constantly adjust the rudder to account for variations in current and wind patterns to reach the desired destination. Similarly, purpose is a malleable intention, constantly adjusting to circumstances and needs.

Strong leadership comes from constantly seeking the best pathway—the clearest, straightest route to fulfilling your calling. Look for opportunities to directly mobilize your passion by seeking value, seeking service, and seeking innovation.

- **Seek Value**: Leaders exist to create value for others. Value is more than economic worth; it measures usefulness and importance in people's lives. When someone benefits in a tangible way from the products or services you provide, there is value. Value is a shifting standard in our competitive, fast-changing society. What creates value today is easily forgotten tomorrow. Leaders disrupt markets when needed to make changes necessary to help others live healthier, richer, and more fulfilling lives.

- **Seek Service**: Leaders make life better for all by lighting candles of hope in nights of darkness. They put people first, serving with kindness and courtesy. Jim Rohm said, "Whoever renders service to many puts himself in line for greatness—great wealth, great return, great satisfaction, great reputation, and great joy."[27]

- **Seek Innovation**: Leaders encourage positive change and innovation. Team members are rewarded for taking risks, trying new things, and improving the customer experience. Leaders give others the freedom to succeed and avoid micromanaging. They exude positive expectations, encouraging team members to push their limits and think out of the box.

Leaders embrace the discipline of seeking value, seeking service, and seeking innovation. By asking questions, evaluating options, and probing for solutions, process improvements are natural and continuous. Leaders find the solution before others recognize there is a problem!

A Stretch Purpose

A purpose should stretch your potential. New challenges can be risky and stressful. Human instinct is to go small and avoid rocking the boat. But if you think small, you will miss the big joy of your calling.

A stretch purpose puts all your talents and gifts to work. It takes you out of your comfort zone and into your stretch zone. There is a saying, source unknown: "The best things in life make you sweaty." A stretch purpose forces you to concentrate your efforts and discipline your time.

I encourage you to put your stretch purpose in writing. What would you like to create, achieve, or accomplish? How does your purpose make the world a better place? A purpose statement move you toward your destination faster. Here are some sample purpose statements:

- "My purpose is to create a unique, fun place to eat great food and experience great people."

- "My purpose is to provide a unique, high-value product that builds customer loyalty and affection."

- "My purpose is to serve, teach, and inspire real estate students to reach their potential in life."

- "My purpose is to speak well, live well, and lead well in order to improve human conditions worldwide."

A purpose statement connects calling with daily routine. Your big picture (calling) is imbued in your small daily tasks (purpose). Sometimes, a stretch purpose is so big it can feel intimidating. You may even feel fearful that you have bitten off more than you can chew. If you can dream it and believe it, it is possible. The biggest room in the world is the room for self-improvement. A stretch purpose should be directional, relational, and aspirational:

- **Directional**: The purpose statement steers you toward desired outcomes. As the captain, gathering like-minded people for the journey, you steer the course, helping others to feel and believe that the destination is real and achievable.

- **Relational**: A purpose statement requires you to connect with others in a meaningful, supportive way. The relationships you build become the heart of your leadership effort. They will carry you, encourage you, and stretch you to become your best.

- **Aspirational**: The stretch statement nudges you toward greatness. "Be not afraid of greatness: some are born great, some achieve greatness, and some have greatness thrust upon them," wrote William Shakespeare.[28] A noble purpose statement is the aspiration that pushes you toward greatness.

A calling pulls your heart, while a purpose stretches your brain. Through mobilizing the power of intention, purpose focuses the leader on high priorities. Many leaders confuse activity with achievement. They waste time with shiny digressions and glittering detours.

Serving as president of Toastmasters International in 2011–2012, my stretch purpose grew out of careful reflection and decades of experience in the organization. Toastmasters International is a network of thousands of independent clubs that meet throughout the world. While the dues to join are low, the annual membership turnover is very high. Clubs lose a staggering 35 to 40 percent of their membership each year. My personal purpose became not just recruiting and building new members but nurturing and retaining members! I looked for ways to instill anchors in our organization to grow and retain our valuable members.

I found my purpose in building community. My purpose statement became enriching the worldwide membership experience through cultivating community. I challenged members to learn, grow, and achieve while building a strong support community. The power of purpose reshaped my own leadership journey with a clear focus. As community was nurtured, I saw increased commitment to our worldwide mission. I made it clear that I expected members who were benefiting from our educational and leadership programs to stick around and give something back. My speeches inspired the emotional connections that made our community real. My board work built community. My published articles reinforced community. I strategically avoided activities that did not in some way build our worldwide community.

I monitored my key stakeholders—headquarters staff, board members, district leaders, and members—to ensure quality of community. In my journal, I recorded hundreds of individual member interactions bonding members to the organization. Through the years, members have come back to me and expressed appreciation for my approach. For me, the real validation is seeing members stay involved to gain maximum benefit from the educational program.

A strong purpose statement is often difficult to create, but even more challenging to apply and live by. Why? Creating a personal purpose statement requires insight, discernment, and discipline. As a leader, the decision to move in one direction is a de facto decision not to move in another. The determinative questions for a leader require the allocation of time and resources. Perhaps this is why the process is avoided by many leaders.

Leaders articulate more than general hopes of peace, prosperity, and success. A "hope list" is *hopeless* without a clear purpose to guide you toward achievement. A purpose is rarely accomplished if not in writing. I started writing out my goals when Cavett Robert told me "The faintest pencil is better than the strongest memory."

In his excellent book *The Purpose Driven Life*, Rick Warren states that purpose gives meaning and significance to our lives. I agree. We are all created for a purpose. To fully realize our personal calling, we must discover our stretch purpose and focus on it every day. A disciplined leader exhibits purposeful activity. When the leader follows a clear, unmistakable purpose, others will follow, sometimes out of curiosity.

Focusing the Purpose

Leaders learn to focus energy and attention to achieve a laser-precise purpose. On my twelfth birthday, I received a glass magnifying scope. I was a fan of the fictional character Sherlock Holmes, created by author Sir Arthur Conan Doyle. In the spirit of the mythical sleuth, I used my new gift to investigate the world—grasshoppers, caterpillars, worms, and other creatures. I spent many happy days on my knees in the backyard of our Hinsdale, Illinois, home, magnifying a world hidden to the naked eye.

It didn't take long for my neighbor Kevin to pay me a visit. He arrived one sunny afternoon and asked to play with my magnifying scope. Holding the scope high in the air, he focused it on a blade of grass. To my surprise, the lens burned a laser-sharp fire in the grass. We both jumped in fear as the fire grew. The seemingly harmless magnifying scope had extraordinary power. When tilted at just the right angle, the scope concentrated the sun's rays in one place instead of many, gathering divergent light photons into a single spot and creating a concentration of heat that could burn virtually anything. My seemingly benign toy became a powerful precision-cutting device.

A leader with laser focus has unlimited potential. I learned this as a freshman at the University of California, Berkeley, playing on the water polo team. Our coach was a legend in the water polo world—Peter J. Cutino. Coach Cutino had a muscular, stocky frame and a bald head. He embodied intentional, purposeful leadership. His calling was coaching, and his purpose was teaching excellence to young men. Every word, every action, every practice had a specific purpose. Nothing was wasted. We swam laps to build endurance. We listened to lectures to refine strategy. We drilled to simulate the most difficult, exhausting, and stressful game scenarios. Even social and recreational activities had a specific purpose. I never wondered why we were doing things.

As a freshman, I was sucking water one day in the deep end of the pool, struggling to survive another grueling Coach Cutino workout. I felt myself slipping closer to the bottom of the pool each minute. Breathing was a luxury. Cutino noticed me and pulled me aside. He said, "Notaro, listen to me. You are barely on this team. Did you know that?! You see those other players out there?" He gestured across the pool to the rest of the team. "They are faster than you! They are quicker than you! They are stronger than you! You need to worker harder! Do you understand that?"

Coach Cutino posted a large sign on the front of his office that read "Is it tough enough?" He was constantly exhorting players to do more, be more, and become more. The better the player, the more energetic the coach's admonition.

While his style appeared harsh to outsiders, he was actually a kind and endearing man. His uncompromising discipline reinforced his winning purpose.

What were the results? Coach Cutino built an extraordinary winning culture. In his twenty-six years as head coach at CAL, his teams won eight NCAA titles. He is recognized as the winningest coach in US water polo history. He served as Olympic coach for Team USA. The Peter J. Cutino Award established in his honor is presented annually to the top American male and female collegiate water polo players. He graduated hundreds of young men from CAL with the tools necessary to succeed in life. I was one of them.

Purpose to Vision

Coach Cutino had an aggressive, bold style, which never obscured his clarity of vision. He saw the pool, the players, and the potential of every game. He knew the opposition and visualized the essential triggers to create the outcome he desired. As a player, I felt my self-limiting beliefs dissolve, replaced by a picture of team success. Coach had a resolute mental toughness. He helped every player imagine not only what was possible but what was probable and expected.

We live in a visual society, and most people need to see and feel a leader's vision before they can connect with the leader's purpose. Vision comes from the Latin verb *videre*, which means *to see, look at, consider*. Vision is much more than just ordinary physical sight; it is the art of envisioning the future in living color as a possible, probable reality. It is seeing further and wider than others. Leaders spring geysers of goodwill, turning scars into stars. They use their calling and purpose to refine and illuminate an appealing, collective vision for all to embrace.

Think of great leaders who embodied their vision. John F. Kennedy imagined sending a man to the moon. Dr. Martin Luther King Jr. imagined a world with little children judged by the conduct of their character, not the color of their skin. Early Bay Colony settler John Winthrop looked as the Massachusetts coast and said, "We will be as a city upon a hill. The eyes of all people are upon us."[29] Leaders excel when they create a vision that encapsulates uncommon longings and desires.

A vision is like an engaging movie trailer that tells the audience to stay tuned for the excitement to come. A well-crafted vision moves the spirit. Michelangelo's epic sculpture *David* is a masterpiece that has stirred millions. I marvel at the ability of the sculptor to visualize perfect form and features within a shapeless block. Similarly, leaders see a perfect vision waiting to break out in the world. Brilliance is a byproduct of a compelling vision.

"To choose a direction, an executive must have developed a mental image of the possible and desirable future state of the organization. This image, which we call a vision, may be as vague as a dream or as precise as a goal or a mission statement," said Warren Bennis.[30] Vision keeps me toiling toward success when my motivation wanes. I once swam a ten-mile six-man relay race in the frigid waters of Lake Tahoe. It was easy to keep the team motivated early in the race or when the finish line came into view; the hardest part was keeping the vision alive through lonely miles five, six, and seven when the finish seemed a long way off.

A leader without an engaging vision is a lonely island in an ocean of opportunity, doomed to forever wander and fail. Yogi Berra said, "If you don't know where you're going, you might not get there."[31] Leaders know a clear vision is the key to keeping people excited and engaged. Sadly, some leaders avoid the process of creating a vision altogether. Without clear direction, followers are forced to choose between multiple priorities. They choose the most appealing—not the most important—priorities, wasting vital resources that are lost forever.

Growing a Vision

Vision is the upward arc that pulls teams to excellence. But walk into any organization and you will see a sanitized vision statement posted in the lobby that looks and sounds good but does very little to motivate results. Why? Many leaders try and push their vision of greatness on others, but it rarely works. "The task of leadership is not to put greatness into humanity, but to elicit it, for the greatness is already there," said John Buchan.[32]

To create a meaningful vision, the leader must engage contributions from all team members. As a frequent leadership speaker, I often field questions from aspiring leaders struggling to craft a vision. "How can I get others to believe in my vision?" they ask. My responses are simple: "Have you engaged others in building the vision?" and "Do *you* believe in your team enough to let them help build the vision?" Casting an effective leadership vision requires cooperation, not coercion. Team engagement precedes team empowerment.

I learned this lesson when I volunteered to lead a one-day nonprofit professional conference with an expected attendance of 300 people. After securing a quality conference venue, I set about engaging committee chairs to assist with the conference. I spent weeks calling and emailing potential volunteers. I thought I had a clear purpose and engaging vision for the team. How wrong I was. Nobody was interested in responding or helping. *Maybe I have the plague*, I worried. The more I asked, the more I was rejected. With deadlines approaching, I was still the only person helping with the conference!

Since nothing was working, I decided to try something new: I recruited a half-dozen attendees to meet and discuss the conference with no strings attached. After introductions, I asked for suggestions on the conference theme: "What is our conference theme?" To my surprise, the room was silent. Nobody spoke a word. The silence lasted for several minutes. Then someone chirped, "You are handling this all wrong, Michael. It is the job of the leader to choose the conference theme! Nobody has ever asked us to make suggestions for the conference theme."

In that moment, I realized the problem: In the past, leaders had dictated how the conference would run, including the theme, speakers, food, keynote, educational presenters, etc. Committee members had felt disrespected because all the decisions had been made for them by the top brass. I knew that needed to change.

"This time we will choose the theme together," I announced. All eyes looked at me with amazement.

"Are you serious?" one asked.

"Yes, I am serious."

After another minute of silence, people started suggesting ideas. Soon, the room was ablaze with suggestions and discussion. Everyone had ideas for the conference theme. We worked collectively to build a collective "we" vision, not a "me" vision. By the end of the meeting, we not only had an appealing conference theme but also an agreement on the speakers, food, and venue. The conference committee was off and running. One member remarked, "This really is *our* conference."

For me, the conference committee created an epiphany moment. The "aha!" moment occurred when I stopped pushing my own rigid expectations and released and trusted others to achieve our common objectives. When team members play a part in creating their own collective vision, they feel buy-in and accomplish much more than they otherwise would. Some leaders demand obedience to a selfish vision that fails to include others. They haggle, drive, and offend others, resulting in bitterness, anger, and ill will.

Visioneering is a team sport that grows organizational capacity. Grow a "we" vision by gathering like-minded resources. Set clear expectations. Listen carefully to team members; everyone's input is expected and valued. Not every suggestion must be embraced, but all contributions must be appreciated. Build future dreams person by person, creating a tapestry vision that motivates collective action. Crafting a "we" vision does not mean you give up your calling or purpose. Quite the contrary! It means you engage others to help in charting the course.

The Vision Magnet

Vision acts as a magnet to pull people and resources together. When a vision is challenging, it attracts resilient people. When a vision is inspiring, it attracts positive people. When a vision is compelling, it attracts dedicated people. The vision often becomes synonymous with the leader. Think of the late Steve Jobs, who made us believe that anything was possible.

Maintaining a magnetic vision requires a flexible mindset. A vision is a living, breathing picture of a future reality. While the present is constantly changing, so is our image of the future. The vision must constantly adjust to meet emerging challenges. When the vision becomes stale, it is time to rally fresh perspectives on achieving your calling. Foresight is looking ahead and considering the forces that may assist or detract from fulfilling your calling. Always keep your vision relevant, empowering, and appealing. While serving on the executive board of Toastmasters International, we revised our envisioned future "to be the first-choice provider of dynamic, high-value, experiential communication and leadership skills development."[33] The new vision provided excitement and clarity for our organization: The world would come to us for dynamic, high-value skill development.

An enduring vision must also be selfless. If the leader promotes a vision that just creates personal benefit, it is bound to fail. Effective leaders go the extra mile to serve others, and they are willing to sacrifice self for the betterment of others. The authentic sacrifice of a leader increases the magnetic appeal of the vision. For instance, Nelson Mandela was a young South African lawyer who spearheaded a vision for dismantling his country's colonial apartheid system. Rising to power thorough the African National Congress in the early 1950s, he represented the vision of millions of engaged and supportive followers. In 1962, he was tried for treason and spent twenty-seven years in prison.[34] He was released in 1990 during a time of escalating civil strife and was finally elected president of South Africa from 1994 to 1999.[35] His personal sacrifice became a magnet, increasing the power and appeal of his vision.

As organizations mature, they often lose sight of their vision. Bad habits proliferate. Departments operate as competitive silos with little sense of the larger collective goals. Employees go through the motions to take a paycheck. Bureaucratic red tape, complacency, and mediocrity drop leaders into a quagmire of confusion. Complaints abound, while initiative and vitality are lost. Afraid to communicate a vision, discouraged leaders offer discouraging, half-baked visions. But a half-baked vision is like a half-baked loaf of bread that is miserable to eat: flat, stiff, and flavorless.

Challenge your team to grow the vision, own the vision, and live the vision. The integrity of a vision is tested daily by human interactions. When team members strive together to achieve success, the vision is taken seriously. In every organization, there are those with good intentions who pull others toward a negative, harmful path. A rogue individual aiming toward failure is a harmful cancer cell. Leaders confront problem people early to avert divisive squabbles and disputes.

Leaders who never create and communicate a vision spend their lives picking up crumbs, drifting aimlessly from one empty pursuit to the next. The best way to guarantee failure in leadership is to never develop an engaging and clear vision.

Summary

Purpose is a steering mechanism that helps you engage fully in your calling. Without a purpose, leaders drift in aimless circles. A clear but flexible purpose provides tracks to run on. Leaders learn to seek value, seek service, and seek innovation. Make time for reflection in crafting a forward-leaning purpose. Look inward to recognize, appreciate, and release available resources. A purpose should be aspirational, relational, and directional. A leader with laser focus has unlimited potential. Create a stretch purpose that is impossible to achieve without outside support.

While purpose is the heartbeat of an organization, vision is the spark. Vision inspires team members to do more, be more, and have more. Never impose a vision; *grow* a vision. Collaborate with team members to build a compelling, inclusive vision that keeps everyone informed, engaged, and energized. The greater the level of team buy-in, the greater the commitment to success. Promote a "we" vision to attract people and resources. Constantly build awareness by growing, sharing, and fulfilling the "we" vision while making adjustments as necessary.

Build purpose and vision as your foundation for leadership success. Together, they will help you recruit the right people and grow excitement for your calling. When achievements are recognized, celebrate important milestones, and keep reading. The next chapter shows you how to align passion, purpose, and vision to create a powerful leadership impact!

4 POWER

A calling is a powerful and creative force. In the first chapter of the Book of Genesis, God called the world into existence, separating light from darkness and land from water in the ultimate exercise of power. Each of us has an inner power that calls us to creative expression, separating love from hate, excellence from mediocrity, and diligence from sloppiness. When you recognize your calling, cultivate your calling, and act on your calling, a dynamic force emerges. It is the real power of you.

Do you wish you had more power? As a young adult, my leadership attempts were often frustrated. It always seemed I lacked the resources, motivation, and support to achieve my goals. Leadership felt like grinding saw dust. In reality, I was operating outside my strength zone and ignoring my natural calling. I was good at trying everything except what I was intended to do, and I never found my groove. Have you ever felt that way? When you operate outside of your calling, mediocre results are predictable.

Leadership power is the ability to leverage strengths and minimize weaknesses; that power can be exploited for positive or malevolent purposes. Political leaders like Hitler, Stalin, and Mao Zedong used political power during the twentieth century to kill millions of their own people. Throughout history, misguided leaders have used power to demean, denigrate, and divide. In contrast, a called leader uses power to unite, inspire, and uplift positive change in the world.

How do you find the power to lead? Stand in your truth. Your truth is what you hold most sacred and dear. It is the foundation of your life and bigger than your job, status, income, or weight. Truth balances and invigorates life, anchoring a calling in a firm place that is not dependent on external validation. If you had one truth to live by, what would it be? Love, service, charity, and freedom are enduring truths only if they are meaningful for you.

Standing in *your* truth reveals your highest and best self. In construction, truing is the process of positioning something to make it balanced or level. When you stand in your truth, you perfectly balance calling, passion, and purpose to produce power. Energy flows where attention goes. Power radiates outward from a solid, balanced truth within. This chapter will show you how to stand in your truth and release your natural charisma within.

Discover Your Truth

"The mass of men lead lives of quiet desperation," said Henry David Thoreau.[36] Most of us have hurried and frenetic lives that leave little time for discovering our truth. Personal dreams remain buried within, waiting for discovery. Often, well-meaning parents and friends push us to pursue expedient goals, instead of the things we really want, need, and desire. You might pursue a career in engineering instead of art because the job prospects are better. You might buy things, go places, and do things just to please and satisfy others. Break free of the disease to please. Truth calls us to resist external pressures, remove the mask, and embrace our honest self. By embracing truth, you ignite the organic call of the leader, which naturally attracts others to your vision.

Finding your personal truth is often uncomfortable. Everyone has a unique power position. The difference between finding your truth and living in falsehood is the difference between night and day. Strangely, we refuse to accept anything but the truth in accounting and science. Why should we expect anything different in leadership?

I once coached a young leader named Richard, who had extraordinary potential. He was a large, bright, burly man with a warm smile and a sincere desire to help people. In a prior career, he had excelled in professional theatre roles as Macbeth, King Lear, and Caesar. While a confident thespian, Richard was failing as a leader. He was overwhelmed with tension, self-doubt, and even depression. When asked to speak in public before groups of any size, he began shaking, quivering, and sweating like a pig. Anxiety reduced this brawny man to a powerless dwarf.

One day I asked Richard what he thought about himself. "There is not much to say about me," he said sheepishly. "I do not have anything to offer myself or others." Richard had a low self-esteem that hindered his growth and performance as a leader. I worked with Richard to peel back decades of rejection and reconnect with his best self. To my surprise,

Richard revealed a passion for serving disabled and disadvantaged children. This was his real leadership calling. When he stood in his truth, he was a new man, confident and powerful. He leveraged his passion to thrive as a leader.

Personal introspection and experience will help you uncover your personal truth. Here are some questions to assist with the process:

- "What personal achievement has brought me the most joy?"
- "What is true for me even when everything around me fails?"
- "What is my highest good in the world?"
- "What false realities diminish my effectiveness?"
- "What skill do I have that most people lack?"
- "When in life have I felt most energized?"

Richard was comfortable performing as someone else but not himself. Acting was a comfortable crutch. Living through the body, voice, and spirit of another, Richard was innocent and safe. But standing in his truth required him to drop his mask, release his inhibitions, and perform as Richard. Sadly, many spend their entire lives acting. Like Richard, the thought of revealing and playing themselves is terrifying.

Have you ever played the role of somebody else? Many feel the pressure to conform to external standards that blunt our power and creativity. From an early age, we obey, imitate, and adapt to others. Our parents direct us through school, telling us what to become. Our professors direct us through college, telling us what to become. Our boss directs us through work, telling us where to go. Soon, a life of conformity is over, and we regret never acting with authenticity.

I challenged Richard to STAND: Seek Truth And New Direction. When we stand, we rise to an erect posture and learn to support ourselves. Standing is holding the course without faltering or fleeing. Richard stood in the authenticity of his real self. He became the leader he was meant to be. Richard defined his truth by revealing things he already knew about himself. Sadly, fear of judgment and denial had buried his dreams deep in the abyss. Reflecting on the source of your truth through mediation, journaling, and speaking it out will bring you in touch with these important feelings.

My favorite TV show as a boy was *Superman* because he had superpowers. X-ray vision and clairvoyance got me excited. When you find your truth, you become a leadership superpower. Standing in your truth elicits super strength. You may not be able to fly, become invisible, bend steel, manipulate time, or leap tall buildings, but there is *one thing* you can do better than everyone else on the planet. What is it? Maybe you are a creator, healer, designer, builder, giver, or teacher. A calling connects talent, experience, and passion to create a superpower within.

Most of the great leaders in history followed an evolutionary journey to finding their truth. Abraham Lincoln began his political career by expressing moral opposition to slavery. He supported the Republican Party's platform in 1850 that limited the expansion of slavery. Although often attacked as an abolitionist, Lincoln believed slavery could be slowly eliminated through gradual emancipation and voluntary colonization, instead of immediate termination. But Lincoln stood in his truth when it mattered most: He signed the Emancipation Proclamation on January 1, 1863, using his war powers to free slaves in states still in rebellion. Immediately, the status of over 3 million Southern slaves was transformed. By standing in his truth, Lincoln found a power that altered the path of history.

Sometimes, the leaders who find their truth and make an impact remain anonymous. I think of the turbulent 1989 Tiananmen Square protests in China when a lone, unnamed Chinese man wearing a white shirt blocked a column of red army tanks driven down Chang'an Avenue. His image was broadcast to a disbelieving world. Although physically weaker than the tanks, he found a source of genuine power by standing in his truth, blocking tons of steel, and changing the course of history. "One resists the invasion of armies; one does not resist the invasion of ideas," said Victor Hugo.[37]

Presidential Truth

Serving as president of Toastmasters International in 2011–2012 pushed me to discover my truth in an unexpected way. I visited numerous Toastmasters districts around the world, which usually climaxed with a conference attended by 200–800 local Toastmasters. Private time is used to coach and problem-solve with the district leaders. Often, by the time a president is known and trusted, his or her year is over, and it is time to welcome the next president.

During one early district visit, I experienced cautious respect but something short of full trust from the members. I could understand their hesitancy. Most of the members and districts I visited did not know me personally; their familiarity came only through my public speeches, a potential meeting at the international convention, and my magazine articles.

Prior to a planned presidential district visit, Toastmasters staff called me and said a prominent professional speaker—who was also a Toastmaster—wanted to schedule me for an extra paid speaking event. I followed up on the request and called the individual, who explained he was not just a speaker but a speech promoter. He had discovered I was a practicing attorney and had taken the liberty of promoting me as the keynote speaker for a professional seminar for lawyers and judges—and would pay me handsomely for a day of public speaking. It sounded too good to be true; I would make more money from a day of speaking than I had paid for my first car! Nothing in Toastmasters rules prevented me from receiving supplemental speaking income. I was interested, but I told the promoter I would think about it and call him back.

While the invitation sounded appealing, I realized my time in that district was limited. Spending a lucrative day in professional speaking would deprive many local Toastmasters of an opportunity to meet a Toastmasters International president. For some, this could be the lost opportunity of a lifetime. As a new Toastmaster, I had met former international president John Noonan in the fall of 1989 when he had visited my home district. I promised local Toastmasters I would be available for them. Speaking at the judicial conference would require me to break my promise to local Toastmasters.

After further consideration, I declined the well-paid speaking opportunity and used my time as planned to mentor district leaders. In that moment, I felt a surge of personal power. I was standing in my truth, despite potential consequences. When I called and told the speech promoter of my decision, he became livid and angrily demanded that I provide an explanation. He said he was losing money and was "ashamed" to be associated with Toastmasters and me. Despite his fury, I held fast to my decision.

When I arrived at the district, the tension was palpable. There was an early meet-and-greet reception with me—the international president. To my surprise, the speech promoter showed up and introduced himself. Given his prior outburst,

I was shocked to meet him face-to-face and did not know what to expect.

"I wanted to meet you personally," he said, "because I could not believe people like you really exist."

"My purpose in visiting the district as international president is not to make money," I explained. "I am sorry it did not work out as you hoped."

The entire exchange played out before local Toastmasters, who watched with amazement. The locals knew the speech promoter by his high-pressure tactics, but they were curious how I would handle the situation. When I said yes to Toastmasters and no to the speech promoter, I established a bond of trust with our members. More importantly, I was *standing in my truth.*

Leadership power came from revealing my truth. When word got out that my commitment to our members was greater than my desire for personal profit, I gained a new level of member acceptance. My motives and mission were clear. Members knew the highest office was bigger than speaking fees, but it took the actions of an international president to validate that knowledge. I felt a trust dividend as members jumped on board quickly and easily with my initiatives. Moreover, I noticed a subtle change in the way members addressed me. Instead of being called "the president," I was called "*our* president." I could have spoken for hundreds of hours on the importance of integrity in leadership, but it would not have had the same powerful effect. Actions speak louder than words!

Speaking your truth gets you in the mindset to take action. It may start with a whisper, which grows into a shout. Speaking truth gets the word out and lets others know what you stand for. You gain courage by speaking truth, growing truth, and living truth. Do it in a kind and gentle way, and you will set yourself apart as a strong and memorable leader.

Believe, Believe, Believe

Lack of belief in self is a looming obstacle that stifles and cripples many leaders. Do you believe in yourself? "The number one problem that keeps people from winning in the United States today is lack of belief in themselves," said Arthur Williams Jr.[38] Belief is a state of mind that holds something to be true. If we believe something to be true, we are instantly empowered and strengthened in its realization.

Sadly, most people find it easier to believe in others than themselves. When you board an airplane, you *believe* the captain is qualified to fly. When you contact the police, you *believe* they will respond to stop crime and injustice. When you dine at a local restaurant, you *believe* the food is safe to eat. Yes, we instinctively believe in others.

Believing in yourself is not easy. For many of us, it requires overcoming decades of negativity, discouragement, and failure. Millions of people are paralyzed by addictions and tragedy. But to thrive as a leader, you must believe in your calling, believe in your resources, and believe in your potential:

- **Believe in Your Calling**: Believe and act on your calling. Draw inner confidence from knowing you are unique and special. No other leader has your unique skill-and-talent mix. Belief allows the natural energy to flow naturally. A crimped garden hose blocks water pressure from flowing to the nozzle head. When you straighten the hose, the water suddenly flows freely outward. Similarly, when you believe in your calling, the inner flow is released to do powerful things in the world. Believing in your calling requires leaning into action with self-assurance and confidence. How much stronger would your belief in yourself be if you knew you could not fail?

- **Believe in Your Resources**: Believe that you will attract the people, money, and ideas necessary to bring your dreams to fruition. Called and committed leaders naturally attract the resources to succeed, as resources emerge from the most unexpected of places. I have met lifelong partners from chance sales calls and appointments. Build a team of emerging leaders committed to growing and serving others. Leaders make the best of every opportunity for learning, networking, and investment, while boosting future resources for success.

- **Believe in Your Potential**: Believe in what you can do. The biggest room in the world is the room for improvement. Leaders envision a glorious future. They see big potential, big results, and big service before others think it is possible. Napoleon Hill said, "Whatever the mind of man can conceive and believe, it can achieve."[39] Real belief comes from recognizing that each person has unique gifts and abilities waiting for expression. When you refuse to accept anything but your best, the mediocre will dissolve before you.

Belief reframes uncertainty with self-assurance, generating self-confidence and power. Alice Walker said, "The most common way people give up their power is by thinking they don't have any."[40] Quite simply, if you never believe in yourself, you will never mobilize the power to achieve your dreams. Attainment comes in *can's*, not *cannot's*.

Charisma Power

One day last fall, my electric dryer died. After seven years of dutiful service, my aging Maytag appeared ready for the appliance graveyard on Halloween night. After a little shopping on the internet, I soon found a promising high-tech replacement. Before purchasing, I made a final check of the old machine and realized the trick was on me: The power plug was hanging loose from a "spooky" socket. The "spooky" socket was a loose electrical socket. Performance was impossible without a consistent connection to the power source.

When leaders believe in themselves and those around them, they have a strong and stable power source. Charisma emerges as a special magnetic charm or appeal.[41] Charisma expresses the human qualities of a called leader. More than white teeth, a radiant smile, or an expensive suit, charisma is a divinely gifted strength derived from the Greek word *charis*, which means *grace*. Each of us has a divinely conferred strength. Becoming the leader you are meant to be is finding your endowed and graceful strength. This is your divinely conferred authority to lead and influence others.

While power is *standing* in your truth, charisma is *revealing* your truth. The supernatural endowment of a charismatic leader is authenticity. By being true to your best self, a source of charismatic strength emerges that creates momentum for the leader. Sadly, many guarded leaders try to hide their charisma.

"Lighten up, Michael. You are way too stiff and serious," said my friend Joanne during a leadership meeting at the Bellevue Club in Oakland, California. "You need to relax and smile more naturally."

Joanne was helping me with my campaign for Toastmasters International office, and I knew she was right. The common charisma blockers of perfectionism, pride, and ego were standing in my way. With a little help, I pruned away those blockers, along with their pesky cousins worry, anxiety, and tension. I became physically comfortable leading out loud, and my campaign flourished.

The presence of charisma explains why two people with similar education, experience, and ability achieve vastly different results. One becomes CEO, while the other stagnates in middle management or fails entirely. Charisma drives leadership promotion. In contrast, lack of charisma invites obscurity. I have found that a leader with charisma and no skills will always rise higher than a leader with skills and no charisma. Charisma is released by presence, personality, and projection:

- **Presence**: Charismatic people have an unmistakable presence. When they walk in the room, the room gets bigger. They are self-assured, confident, and own the space around them. Like a powerful magnet, others are naturally attracted to them. They are poised and self-reliant, buoyed by assurance of their values and beliefs, while remaining solidly engaged and present for others. They are both anchored and engaged, living in the moment reacting, responding, and shaping the mood around them. Think of Margaret Thatcher or Pope Francis.

- **Personality**: Charisma is more than a fleeting "star" quality; it is an enduring "you" quality that makes you interesting and appealing. Charismatic people have a passion for life that is infectious. They exude a love for life that invites others to be a part of it. An engaging, vibrant personality radiates outward from an inner passion for life. They are simply fun to listen to, regardless of their topic. Think of actor Will Smith or basketball great Charles Barkley.

- **Projection**: Charismatic leaders project appealing eye contract, body language, and facial expressions. Inner assurance reveals outward confidence. Ordinary exchanges become exhilarating personal experiences. The warm public presence forges an emotional bond with others. Think of Oprah Winfrey or Ronald Reagan.

Charismatic people differ widely in their style and approach. Since charisma is personal, each of us projects our presence and personality in a unique way. The power in charisma is caring for others. When the leader cares, they become charismatic to you. A charismatic singer, speaker, or salesman is hard to miss. They draw you in, sharing love with their eyes, voice, and touch. We want to see more, feel more, and catch a piece of what they have. This explains millions of Twitter feeds for charismatic celebrities. Charisma opens heads, hearts, and pocketbooks.

You will never thrive as a leader if you do not feel comfortable in your own skin. When you are comfortable internally, you project comfort externally. Charismatic leaders develop the inner strength to radiate attention away from themselves toward others. Charisma is naturally modulating your voice, moving your body purposefully, and aligning verbal and nonverbal cues.

The foundation for charisma is a healthy self-concept. Some leaders are fortunate to naturally possess a winning self-concept. I was not one of them. It took me many years of seeking and nurturing the call of the leader. Ultimately, I developed personal charisma in the last place I thought I would find it: when I stopped emulating others and started believing in myself.

True charisma draws others out before you speak a word. Your body language is open and inviting. Charisma is a bountiful fountain that spills over and warms the heart. It is emotional wealth pouring from a deep internal reservoir. Charisma produces the confidence to connect and influence others. Their charm makes you feel good about yourself. The charismatic person is comfortable in who they are to make you comfortable in who you are.

Charismatic leaders exude gravitas. Their words are measured and weighty. They possess the influence, resources, and ability to make a difference in the world. Thomas Hobbes wrote, "The power of a man ... is his present means, to obtain some future apparent good."[42] Think of the Dalai Lama or Billy Graham.

Developing charisma is less about trying to impress others and more about listening to and engaging others. Many years ago, I spent months researching new cars and finally decided to buy an Infiniti luxury sedan. I confirmed the choice was a good one, since both my mom and aunt drove Infinitis. I made an appointment with a salesman at a local dealership in anticipation of buying my new car. When I arrived, the salesman asked a few questions and gave me a test drive. I was sold. I loved the car even more after the test drive, and the price was great. We met in a small conference room to finalize the deal. As the salesman talked, I kept waiting for him to present a sales contract for me to sign, but it never came. He kept talking and talking and talking. One hour later, with no contract, I reached a breaking point. I did not want a new car anymore. My old one was just fine. I demanded that the salesman let me out of the room. The salesman had wasted so much effort trying to impress, that the sale had slipped away.

The call of the leader is less about impressing people and more about empowering people. Charismatic people are good listeners. They are sensitive to the vibe in the room. Instead of impressing others, they serve and engage others. After recovering from my imprisonment with the gregarious Infinity salesman, I decided it was time to continue my search for a new car. I wandered into a Hyundai dealership and joyfully leased a grey Sonata from a bumbling Hyundai salesman. He forget his sales presentation, forgot the model features, forgot where he kept the key, forgot the price, and even forgot my name, but his endearing eyes of compassion and humility made me laugh at each mistake. We laughed together, and before I realized it, I had leased a new car— and loved the experience. A few years later, I went back to the same salesman and leased a new model.

A leader with presence radiates energy and connection in his foibles. Mistakes are just bumps on the road to success. They make the leader human, since we all make mistakes. The Infinity salesman offended me. The Hyundai salesmen engaged me. He made me feel good about the buying experience, regardless of how the words came out (or maybe in spite of them).

Power-Up Charisma

Charismatic leaders demonstrate physical power through nonverbal communication. Over 65 percent of communication is derived from nonverbal communication.[43] Body movement, arm gestures, vocal tone, and facial expressions resonate directly with the inner brain. Nonverbal communication is essential in establishing trust. Here are some important ways to increase your physical charisma:

1. **Look Up**: Look up at people when you speak. Looking down or avoiding eye contact reflects a poor self-image. Eye contact shows interest and attention, revealing personal thoughts, emotions, and feelings. There is a saying (source unknown) that the eyes are the windows to the soul. When your soul is revealed, an authentic connection/bond grows. People with higher levels of eye contact are perceived as more personable, powerful, and trustworthy. Real eye communication is more than an occasional peep or fleeting glance. Practice eye communication with everyone with whom you speak, and your connection and influence will grow.

2. **Stand Up**: Your physical presence projects victory or defeat. A firm, erect posture is necessary to project your energy outward. Stand with feet shoulder-width apart in an athletic position, with your weight leaning forward. Communication flows on smooth, forward energy. Nothing telegraphs failure like a dropping, hunched bearing. Leaders often try appearing casual by leaning to one side or the other, which rarely works. Stop hunching, bending, or leaning. Lift the top of your chest off your pelvis, tuck in your abdomen, and breath from the diaphragm. To improve your posture, try the Miss America exercise: Stand with your back straight against the wall and move forward while balancing a hardback book on your head. Having problems balancing? Be patient and keep practicing as you release the blocked energy of your persona.

3. **Speak Up**: Charismatic people dial up the vocal energy to engage others. A mumbling monotone defuses energy and puts people to sleep. Speak up and make your speech dynamic. Dale Carnegie tells the story of a student who was a boring speaker.[44] "Pretend you are punched in the face and have something to say to your assaulter," challenged Carnegie. Suddenly, the meek,

timid student became dynamic and eloquent, speaking in his own defense. Just by changing his attitude, he became a dynamic speaker. Carnegie's message was simple: Believe in what you say and say it with passion.

4. **Smile Up**: Lift your facial muscles (apples) and smile up. There is nothing more appealing than an open and warm smile. Smiling shows people you like them. Some of us have a neutral or stern facial expression and need to practice smiling. Open your mouth, lift your cheekbones, and practice smiling. How powerful is smiling? For years, I have listened to one of America's most successful pastors on the radio and never realized why Joel Osteen is so successful. Then I saw him in person and instantly realized the reason: He is the "smiling pastor," who preaches an entire sermon without losing his smile! Smile in a natural way. Open your mouth and turn up the corners. Let your teeth shine through (and clean them, if necessary).

5. **Dress Up**: Dress and appearance shape first impressions, which are lasting. Amazingly, tests show people will assume your education, status, and income based on how you groom and dress yourself. Dress appropriately for the position you seek. When in doubt, err on the side of dressing up, not down. If you don't have a natural knack for selecting fashionable clothing (like me), choose a trusted friend to assist you while you shop. Shape your attire to be just a little bit nicer than your audience. With some intentional effort, your wardrobe can reflect the best of who you are.

Dial up charisma by doing things to perk up your energy. Listen to your favorite song or watch your favorite music video to establish the right vibe. I listen to a favorite comedy routine from Brian Regan that is silly and puts me in a fun mood. The people I lead have fun when I have fun. Find a way to source and release your personal energy. Charisma is contagious, but it must begin inside of you.

Warm, open, and inviting body language makes the leader appealing. While many leaders burn out, charismatic leaders regenerate with power. They monitor themselves, knowing how they are perceived by others. Charisma aligns with calling by connecting with followers at a deeper emotional level. Followers bond to who you are as much as what you do.

Charisma is blunted when we construct a public façade that protects us from others. The public mask conceals a truthful inner power. We don't want others to see our true self, so we keep talking and talking like the Infinity salesman. The façade may conceal your worst, but it also conceals your best. It also fuels distrust, because others figure out you are hiding your best.

Getting people onboard and invested in success is a challenging endeavor. Charisma is one trait that will engage people and put them on your team. While you may have a good product, your most important asset is people. Part of charisma is being interesting. While the definition of charisma is floating, the results are not.

Truth Power

The best part of standing in your truth is that every day is a personal celebration. The only standards you live up to are your own. We all like to be associated with leaders who are living out their truth in an honest, ethical, and trustworthy manner. You become the leader everyone wants to emulate.

Most often, we find our truth by discovering what it is not. Spending a few years at a dead-end, unfulfilling job provides a great motivation. We discover an unhappy inner psyche waiting to jump out. That person has lived life to conform to the expectations of what others want and desire. The butterfly emerges from the cocoon when there is a strong enough desire to fly.

Ultimately, people do not join causes; they join leaders they believe in. Leaders with strong character show interest in their employees' lives. They work alongside those they oversee and lend a helping hand when necessary. They help others develop professionally through mentoring and coaching. They are open and authentic, inspiring others to stretch and grow, and supporting them when they fail. The byproduct of a leader with character is trust and loyalty.

My favorite childhood memory was having Sunday dinner with my Italian grandfather. I called him Gramps, since we shared the same name. Of course, the family feast always included a cornucopia of gastronomic delights: lasagna, spaghetti, meatballs, mushroom ravioli, tortellini, and garlic bread. I often ate too much food. One night, I asked Gramps for a third helping of spaghetti.

"Can you eat all that pasta, Michael?"

"Of course I can!" I responded enthusiastically. "Gramps, I am bigger on the inside than I look on the outside."

The power of truth is bigger on the inside than the outside. Leadership is not about being the biggest and loudest; it is about being the deepest and the widest. A leader who pushes too hard often pushes themselves out of leadership. When we touch a heart, we activate a reciprocal principle of appreciation. People who are heard are more likely to hear out our calling—and follow. We grow followers because they like and respect us.

Summary

Where do you find the power to lead? By standing in your personal truth. Truth balances and invigorates your calling, revealing your highest and best self. Truth directs your energy in an impactful way, since energy flows where attention goes. Living in your truth makes you believable, credible, and powerful as a leader.

Discover your truth by finding out what brings you joy, meaning, and energy in life. Listen for the authentic inner voice that reveals truth: the solid ground of humanity. Heed the clearest voice, not the loudest voice. Heed the resolute voice, not the fickle voice. Others will follow a trusted, grounded leader with a noble calling. Make yourself worthy of the trust others have in you.

Seek out mentors and friends who challenge you to STAND (Seek Truth And New Direction) in everything you do. Rise to become the influential leader you are meant to be. Power is more than titles, position, or money. Power is the authority entrusted to you by those you serve. We instinctively trust confident leaders who believe in themselves and believe in us. Learn to believe in your calling, believe in your resources, and believe in your potential.

When leaders believe in themselves, they exude authentic charisma. Charisma drives leadership influence and promotion. It is a natural byproduct of living in your truth, released by your presence, personality, and projection. Take action to become a more confident leader: look up, stand up, speak up, smile up, and dress up.

In the next chapter, we explore courage—the essential quality for leadership greatness. Courage elevates average leaders to unforgettable leaders. Stay tuned!

5 COURAGE

L eadership is inspired, or it is nothing at all. When you feel the passion, purpose, and power of your calling, you are ready to pursue your dreams with gusto. Then reality sets in. "What did I do? Am I crazy?" The voices of self-doubt and fear capture your thoughts. A moment of decision arrives: Will you move forward in courage or retreat in fear?

From the battlefield to the boardroom, effective leaders find the nerve to act bravely in times of danger, dread, or difficulty. Courage is not the absence of fear; it is the ability to act *in spite of* fear. Qualities we admire like discipline, persistence, honesty, and kindness are really byproducts of first acting with courage.

In this chapter, you will learn how to grow inner courage through confronting reality and building strong convictions. Every calling follows a path that tests your attitude and persistence. Without courage, your calling will never be realized. Saying yes to your higher self requires courage. I learned it all from my friend Hien, who taught me the true meaning of courage.

The Call to Freedom

"The bullets whizzed above my head. Angry Communist soldiers shouted over a loud speaker: 'Do you hear me? Turn the boat back now!' I kept my head down and prayed as the threats got louder and louder. Finally, Dad steered our small boat out of Saigon Harbor and into the open sea. I felt the ocean mist—the spray of saltwater in my face. Freedom ... Ah! ... Freedom at last!"

Those passionate words were spoken thirty years ago in a student dining hall by Hien, a Vietnamese immigrant and engineering student at the University of California, Berkeley. His words are as clear to me today as the day he delivered them. Hien felt the call of freedom and risked his life to achieve it. While he spoke with a strong Vietnamese accent, his daring message silenced a room of amazed undergraduates. In the weeks that followed, Hien and I grew to be fast friends. I saw in Hien the power of courage every single day.

Hien's family spent many weeks preparing to escape from Communist South Vietnam. Initially, they discussed the pros and cons. "Should we stay or go? What is the best way to go? When should we go?" Fear threatened to overwhelm the planning, but when the decision was made to escape, nobody wavered. Every family member played a critical role: Hien readied the tiny boat; his dad steered the boat; his mom prepared food provisions; and his sister carried the flashlight and prayed. It was a coordinated team effort. The slightest error would have invited a hail of bullets or a trip to prison. Freedom beckoned, and Hien's family took courageous action and never looked back.

"We build dikes of courage to hold back the flood of fears," said Martin Luther King Jr.[45] Hien and his family believed surrendering to the status quo of Communism denied the essence of their being. They stood strong on their convictions, looked past the convenience of everyday life, and dedicated themselves to reaching a new life of freedom.

As leaders, we rarely face decisions of life or death, like Hien and his family did. But we do face difficult circumstances that require a hardy leadership response. And rarely do those stressful problems and challenges disappear by delay or avoidance. Blaming others, making excuses, or dwelling on a bad predicament only prolongs the agony and usually makes the problems worse rather than better.

Courage is finding your edge—the outer extremity of your comfort zone—and going beyond it. All personal growth comes by pushing out the limits. We can hide, recoil, and retreat, abandoning our dreams, or we can move forward with courage. "Life shrinks or expands in proportion to one's courage," said Anaïs Nin.[46] Bravery is required to fulfill the call of the leader. Are you afraid of a steep drop? Are you afraid of losing control? As a leader, courage keeps you sharp in a competitive world through building emotional, mental, and physical resilience. If Hien's family can endure a perilous journey to freedom, what's stopping *us* from stepping up to achieve our dreams?

Confront Reality

Hien and his family had the courage to confront reality in all of its glory. They knew they could never be happy in a place where basic freedoms were denied. All leaders must face the good, the bad, and the ugly of their organization. If you keep doing what you have always done, you will keep getting what you have always gotten. Many leaders live in the most populous state in the union, the fifty-first state, the state of Denial. Denial is like a tempting opioid that hides the pain of reality. It may feel good for a while, but future decline is inevitable. If you keep kicking the can down the road, you will eventually stub your toe.

Leaders face a myriad of challenges. Sometimes, it is losing money, a toxic culture, a problem employee, or a deteriorating brand. Ignoring the problem will not make it go away. I once had a friend who received a mud facial at a local health spa. He boasted a radiant face for a few days … then the mud started falling off. Leaders who deny reality set themselves up for an embarrassing descent. Why wait for the mud to start falling?

Courageous leaders seek reality, assess reality, and transform reality:

1. **Seek Reality**: Leaders deal with confusion and chaos every day. Beneath the covering of platitudes and puffery, the truth is waiting to be discovered. Learn to gather information on what is really happening as early as possible; ask the tough questions nobody is asking, and listen. Finding reality is crucial to good decision-making and impactful leadership. The truth may be messy and uncomfortable, but it will set you free.

2. **Assess Reality**: Leaders use intuition and analysis to assess the real challenges ahead. The warts and faults of an organization provide the best foundation for planning future success. Engage gifted team members in open and honest dialogue. M. Scott Peck said, "We cannot solve life's problems except by solving them."[47] Use your head

and your heart to assess reality and plan a successful future.

3. **Change Reality**: Leaders are change agents who are constantly working to updating people, products, and processes to achieve optimum results. This can be a frightening reality for the complacent nonperformers. Not all change is progress, but all progress requires change, which makes people uncomfortable. If you face the reality of change, you will change the face of your reality.

During the year I served as president of Toastmasters International, we decided that maintaining the high level of service to our members and implementing our worldwide strategic plan required increasing the dues. We confronted reality and made a difficult solution. Many members were personally outraged with me, and they were not afraid to tell me so. I received scores of angry emails. Critics argued I was ruining Toastmasters. "The cost of Toastmasters [including club dues] is too high," they asserted. While empathizing with members in financial need, I also knew that our organization needed the extra revenue to build staff and continue vigorous growth and quality upgrades. I believed the dues increase was the right decision, and most of the members eventually did, too, as our organization continued to flourish.

You will never scale the peak of prominence until you confront the rock of reality. Here are some questions to help your organization confront reality:

- What is your organization's biggest need?

- How can you increase customer value?

- How can you eliminate customer disappointments?

- How can you distinguish your brand?

- How does your culture impact bottom-line performance?

- Is your mission known both internally and externally?

Confront Bad Habits

For many years, I was not growing as a leader. My results were stagnant, even declining. I was confronting my external reality in all of its glory, but that external reality was not the real problem. I was the problem, reflected in entrenched bad habits that threatened my leadership. Courage is confronting inner demons. When you conquer yourself, everything else is easy by comparison. So take a hard look within and purge the imperfections. Face each obstacle directly—one by one—and resolve to change them.

- **Avoiding Accountability**: Learn to hold all people accountable for their performance (including yourself). Create a culture where people are expected to deliver on their commitments. By setting the example, you hold yourself to the same high standards you expect from others.

- **Blaming Others**: Blaming is a popular modern pastime. When things go wrong, many leaders blame first and ask questions later. Shortsighted leaders blame others to deflect responsibility and soften the impact of their mistakes. But blaming undermines the long-term credibility and competence of the leader. Leaders who blame give away control and diminish their own integrity and authority.

- **Complacency Quicksand**: Sluggish leaders become complacent with the status quo. They stop improving and settle into complacency quicksand. If your organization is not growing and improving, it is probably degrading as you lose your competitive edge. Good enough is never good enough. If the leadership becomes static—resistant to new ideas—the organization hardens from the top, down. Marginal work and shoddy attitudes foreshadow failure.

- **Disconnected Leaders**: Insecure leaders are afraid to network and connect with like-minded leaders. Without a support network, leaders have nobody to turn to when times get hard. Seek professional backing to strengthen your leadership resources. By supporting team members, the leader boosts productivity, improves decision-making, and eliminates blind spots. Every leader needs a strong cadre of advisors providing helpful support.

- **Executive Lording**: Controlling leaders lord over others by micromanaging. While they often pretend to delegate, they refuse to get out of the way, and stifle those doing the work. Grow an environment where people have the freedom to succeed without constant criticism and henpecking. To fully embrace your calling, you must release it to the capable hands of competent associates.

- **Fresh Start**: All of us have an occasional bad hair day. Leaders are no different. Avoid the temptation of clinging to failure or wallowing in your grievances. Make a fresh start each day. Let go of each day so you can make the next one even better.

- **Garnering Kudos**: Give credit to the teammates who make success possible. Avoid demanding personal veneration and praise from every organizational success. As a Toastmasters leader, I learned to take more than my fair share of blame in difficult times and less than my share of credit in successful times.

Many well-intentioned leaders begin with big dreams and aspirations. But they work on everything except themselves. When a key manager quits or a crucial customer becomes irate, your true leadership colors are tested. Leadership is filled with unexpected twists and turns that test our patience and perseverance. The inner resolve of the leader can solve problems or grow them.

Action is essential to confronting reality and conquering the obstacles in your way. It reminds me of the story of the man who lost his job and found himself in financial ruin. He looked up at the heavens and said, "God, I am broke. I have lost my home, my car, and my wife. Please give me a break. Help me win the lottery right now!"

God looked down from Heaven and said, "Give *me* a break, buddy. Buy a lottery ticket."[48]

Leadership is hard work. We must work as hard on improving themselves as building our organization.

Growing Courage

Courage grows from deeply held beliefs. For Hien and his family, freedom was a powerful conviction, an eternal and inviolate faith in their chosen path. Leaders with conviction create stability even in the most troubling times. They radiate self-assurance and attract followers who mirror their emotional state. We naturally gravitate to confident, strong leaders in times of uncertainty and fear. Without conviction, leaders are swept and tossed by the winds of popularity. When things get tough, leaders without conviction dissolve like jelly in an earthquake. Develop your convictions and become a more confident, trusted leader.

Your backbone is close to your heart for a reason: Convictions emanate from the heart. *E-motion*—the energy within—creates motion without. When you know what moves your spirit, it will move others to believe you, trust you, and follow you. Deeply held beliefs create the courage to act. The process of arriving at convictions comes from personal reflection. The root word *convict* means "to prove based on clear evidence."[49] Conviction arises from the things you believe so deeply, you would stake your life on them.

Conviction crosses a personal bridge called *courage*. Some days, you feel that you just cannot do it. There are naysayers, setbacks, and adversities. The blustery wind of negativity threatens to blow you off the bridge! But faith grows through action. You must summon every ounce of your nerve and fortitude to cross over. To prepare for the journey, leaders know their convictions, grow their convictions, and show their convictions:

- **Know Your Convictions**: Determine your convictions by finding what is most true and honorable within. Make time to journal, meditate, and reflect on verifiable truth in your life. By aligning accurate data, personal values, and emotional intelligence, we come to know our convictions. These beliefs form the basis of who you are and what you will become.

- **Grow Your Convictions**: When you know your convictions, you can grow your convictions. Read, study, and associate with people who bring out your firmly held beliefs. Follow your hopeful calling and grow the breadth and depth of your convictions. For instance, if one of your convictions is love, then learn as much as you can about growing love in the world. If one of your convictions is humor, then learn as much as you can about promoting laughter in the world.

- **Show Your Convictions**: Show your convictions by staying the course when things get tough. Convictions provide a strong anchor in a stormy sea. While leadership is uncertain and always changing, the leader who acts from firmly held convictions brings assurance and security. My personal convictions are freedom, service, integrity, and excellence, and my challenge is to live my convictions with certainty but not arrogance, and confidence but not cockiness.

We expect leaders to know what they believe—and why. Leaders who know their convictions, grow their convictions, and show their convictions radiate a magnetic personal strength that attracts followers. Strongly grounded leaders attract followers who are more likely to show the strength of their own convictions. The result is a team willing to take calculated risks, accept responsibility, and devote energy to making the world a better place.

Leaders with strong conviction face obstacles with courage and positive resolve. Setbacks are merely necessary milestones on the success highway. While it is tempting to drive past our mistakes at high speed, leaders with conviction have the courage to face each obstacle and learn. They assess how things could be done differently next time.

The Courage to Act

Courage is more than running a dangerous rapid, jumping off a bridge, or climbing a tall mountain. It is hearing the call to leadership, your call to leadership, and doing the very things you avoid most. Without courage, the leader is trapped in a cage of conformity.

Have you ever been in an organization where everyone secretly talks about the real problems, but nobody does anything about them? Discernment and insight alone do not make the leader. The leader is always the one willing to confront reality and take action on the most pressing challenges or opportunities.

For many years, I told my friends and family that I wanted to start a real estate business. I repeated it so often, I sounded like an advertisement. I liked hearing myself talk but was afraid to actually take action, trapped in the paralysis of analysis. What if the economy turned downward? What if the interest rates went up and nobody could afford to buy? What if there were too many commercial real estate agents? I exaggerated the horrible outcomes, concluding I would be homeless and begging for food if I tried.

Fortunately, I was unhappy enough with a former employer to leave and start my own commercial real estate company in 1995. It was the best decision of my life. I increased my happiness and income while reducing my stress. My business thrived, and none of the things I feared happened, although there were plenty of unexpected challenges. In retrospect, I wondered why it had taken so long to act on my dreams.

The call of the leader is saying yes to your higher self. But it also involves saying no to your mundane, average self. Concert musicians practice many hours per day to achieve mastery, and great athletes invest years in rigorous training. The price of leadership is the value of your dreams. The bigger your dreams, the bigger the price you must pay. There is a personal cost, measured in foregone pleasures. There is an immediate financial cost, measured in money invested for future benefit. There is an emotional cost, measured in hopes deferred or denied. There is a physical cost, measured in the blood, sweat, and tears that can never be recovered.

The world changes when a courageous leader takes action on their calling. Leaders who wait for things to happen become reactors, not actors, and lose control of their destiny. Leaders know their goal and gather relevant facts and data while assimilating emotional cues.

Courage grows with methodical, small steps that expand your skills and abilities. Small steps build character. Minor victories reinforce a spirit of conquest. Courage is not a reckless act; it is a valiant act. Leaders fully plan and analyze all options before taking action. They know that strong preparation yields strong results. Reckless action does not display courage. Courage becomes the enduring habit revealed in defining moments. Often, the shining moment is preceded by years of routine service and disciplined commitment. Robert Allen said, "Everything you want is just outside of your comfort zone."[50] Stretch your comfort zone and experience true freedom. I learned that from my friend Hien.

Acts of courage often go unnoticed. You may never get credit for caring acts: mentoring a coworker through troubled times, striving for excellence when mediocrity is acceptable, or transforming a failing business model to make success possible. Courage is a slow, long discipline that will define and refine your leadership brand. Build your courage and transform your life.

Courage Is a Muscle

Visit any local gym and you will see people exercising their muscles. Some are sweating and grunting. Some run on machines, while others run their mouths—standing around and pretending to exercise. But the benefits come only to those who exercise in a disciplined, methodical manner. If you are lifting weights, start with small weights of ten pounds, then go to fifteen pounds, then go to twenty pounds, etc.

Similarly, courage is a mental muscle that is built slowly and methodically. You are not born with courage; you develop it through training and experience. By facing your fear every day, you build courage and confidence. Small acts of courage, repeated consistently, build the courage muscle and shape your destiny. Speak truth to a coworker. Do the right thing, even if it might be criticized. Go someplace new. When you have the courage to face escalating fears, your courage muscle grows exponentially.

Courage is an action word. If you wait for your ship to come in, it may never dock. Swim out and meet the courage craft. When you take action, it triggers like-minded people to gather at your side. Motivated leaders have a bias for action. They are not afraid to fail. They move out of their comfort zone to not only *see* the opportunity but *seize* the opportunity.

As a young Toastmaster, I learned to say yes early and often to leadership opportunities. I wanted people to know that they could count on me to take action. I said yes to public speaking, yes to developing new leaders, and yes to building a positive culture. I said no to anything that would hold me or other leaders back from reaching our potential.

The leader's courage-building routine requires three priorities:

- **Start Courage**: Break the ice by doing something new. "One doesn't discover new lands without consenting to lose sight, for a very long time, of the shore," said André Gide.[51] Take action, despite feeling incapable or unworthy. Overcome the inertia, and it will get a lot easier the second time. Start that business, run a 5K race, call a sales prospect, deliver a speech, stand for office, or take an overseas trip. The second time never comes unless you have start courage.

- **Stay Courage**: Stay courage is persistence. When you stay the high course through difficult times, you not only gain mental discipline but also the trust and admiration of those you serve. It is easy to abandon people and jump ship when times get hard. Stay courage inspires the leaders to hang on through challenges and adversity to enjoy a brighter future.

- **Stop Courage**: Leaders must confront reality and stop things that are not beneficial. Sometimes, this requires a reduction in force, the recall of dangerous products, or the firing of toxic employees. Stop courage eliminates waste, fraud, and neglect. Stop courage is the difficult thing that is the right thing. Stop courage prunes the tree to allow greater growth in the future.

Courage is the toll we pay on the success highway. Leaders must be agile enough to exercise start courage, stay courage, and stop courage as conditions demand. When challenges arise, it is tempting to take the easy route. Courage is the acquired skill that pulls you toward your calling, and multiplies opportunities.

Courage Leads to Greatness

What makes great leaders? Is it wealth, fame, or power? I do not think so. There are plenty of wealthy celebrities who are far from great. Leadership greatness is a rare quality defined by one common quality: resolute moral courage.

Great leaders do the right thing under pressure. They diligently and methodically pursue excellence without demanding attention or cutting corners. They act bravely, even sacrificially, to lift, save, and enrich the lives of those around them. Their greatness lies not in the expanse of people who serve them but in the expanse of people they serve. Of course, all greatness is relative. The more greatness you have, the more relatives you have (if you didn't laugh, you might be taking yourself too seriously!).

Moral courage is a trait that grows from the inside out. Margaret Thatcher, the daughter of a Grantham grocer, had a purpose and sense of personal mission rarely seen in political life. She was Britain's longest-serving prime minister of the twentieth century and the first woman appointed to the position. Trained as a chemist and barrister, she defied the entrenched chauvinism of Britain's political aristocracy with her brilliance and charm. With Britain suffering from high unemployment and economic stagnation, the Iron Lady took bold steps to free labor markets, renew entrepreneurship, and stand up to powerful trade unions. Despite withering criticism, she refused to take an easier, less principled path. As Britain's economy emerged, she gave credit back to the British people. She led Britain to decisive victory in the 1982 Falklands War, survived an assassination attempt in 1984, and is remembered as one of the greatest political leaders of the twentieth century. Her greatness came from her resolute moral courage; she never abandoned her firmly held personal convictions.[52]

Greatness also comes from quiet courage. Chesley "Sully" Sullenberger was a shy boy who grew up with a passion for flying. Growing up in Denison, Texas, Sully built model planes and dreamed of becoming a pilot. He received an appointment to the United State Air Force Academy in June 1969 and graduated in 1973 with the Outstanding Cadet in

Airmanship Award. As military pilot, he advanced through air force tactical and training positions while pursuing a special interest in aircraft accident investigation. After his air force retirement, he was employed by US Airways and its precursor airlines between 1980 and 2010. He continued to study and report on aircraft safety issues. He even studied the psychology of maintaining the aircraft crew through crisis conditions.[53]

On January 15, 2009, Captain Sullenberger was piloting US Airways Flight 1549, taking off from LaGuardia Airport when his plane struck a gaggle of geese, disabling the power in both engines. Sullenberger made a courageous snap decision to forego returning to the airport, and he guided his plane to a water landing on the Hudson River. Miraculously, all 155 passengers were safely rescued. Over forty years and twenty thousand hours of flying experience paid off handsomely when he needed it most. By quietly honing his skills in obscurity, he was ready to shine in a time of crisis. The courage and knowledge to do the right thing under pressure was not accidental; it came from many decades of studying and researching aircraft safety.

Boxing great Joe Frazier discovered greatness through his preparation. He said, "You can map out a fight plan or a life plan, but when the action starts, it may not go the way you planned, and you're down to your reflexes—that means your [preparation]. That's where your roadwork shows. If you cheated on that in the dark of the morning, well, you're going to get found out now, under the bright lights."[54]

Moral courage is the ability to do the right thing under pressure. I call greatness the g-force in leadership. Every pilot strapped into the cockpit of a supersonic jet feels the pull of gravity (the g-force) on takeoff. A powerful acceleration resistance makes every kind of turning or twisting harder.

But some leaders have a unique ability to make gravity work for them, pushing them toward greater heights. They resist the pressure to quit, crumble, or wither, and the g-force moves them to growth, to gratitude, and to giving:

- **Growth**: Great leaders are growing leaders. Captain Sullenberger committed to learning as much as possible about aircraft safety by studying aircraft accidents and how to avoid them. When Flight 1549 was finally recovered from the Hudson Bay, investigators found a small library book packed in Sullenberger's luggage behind the cockpit: Just Culture: Balancing Safety and Accountability.[55] Yes, leaders are readers. Greatness is a byproduct of having the best knowledge, training, and skills when it is needed. Leaders seek personal and professional growth at every opportunity. When a leader stops learning, they stop growing, and greatness escapes them. Each new challenge presents the opportunity for learning more, growing more, and serving more.

- **Giving**: Great leaders are giving leaders. Captain Sullenberger gave generously of his time long before he achieved international acclaim. While flying for US Airways, he volunteered as an air safety instructor and accident investigator, serving on numerous air safety committees for the air force, National Transportation Safety Board (NTSB), and NASA.[56] Leaders lend their expertise, time, money, and influence to make others safer and better. We stand tallest when stooping to help another. Your most valuable gift is your time, and great leaders have the habit of giving generously. When the leader stretches to give their best, others are motivated to do the same.

- **Gratitude**: Great leaders are grateful leaders. Captain Sullenberger remained thankful to the passengers and crew of Flight 1549 for their enormous contributions. As a sought-after speaker and celebrity, he maintained a deep sense of humility and contentment, deflecting attention away from himself. An attitude of gratitude unlocks the fullness of life's calling, the true source of joy and energy. Many leaders focus on what they do not have, rather than being grateful for what they do have. A spirit of praise swings open doors of opportunity. Gratitude generates social capital, growing optimism, loyalty, and trust, forcing us to find goodness in others. Every day is Thanksgiving for the grateful leader.

Greatness is not a crown to wear or throne to sit upon. It is bold action that inspires and empowers others to live fully. The forces of greatness conspire in favor of leaders who pursue their calling with resolute moral courage. When adversity looms, opportunity blooms. G-force is the acceleration resistance that grips every leader at one time or another. Take action on your fear and learn to grow through it, give through it, and praise through it.

Summary

Leaders who risk the least live the least. "The brave may not live forever but the cautious do not live at all," said Meg Cabot.[57] The exciting work of fulfilling your calling requires acting with courage. Courage is the ability to act in spite of fear, and it is the purest validation of a great leader.

Effective leaders confront truth by seeking reality, assessing reality, and transforming reality. They create a positive, supportive culture for all to succeed. Through confronting bad habits, leaders work hardest on improving themselves. They eliminate bad habits like avoiding accountability, blaming others, cozying up with complacency, disconnecting from advisors, executive lording, failing to start fresh, or gobbling excessive praise. Leaders know that personal growth requires courage, and courage springs from acting on deeply held personal convictions. To cross a bridge called courage, leaders must know their convictions, grow their convictions, and show their convictions.

Serious leaders build their courage muscle every day by consistently stepping outside of their comfort zone. They practice start courage, stay courage, and stop courage. Greatness springs from resolute moral courage—doing the right thing under pressure. Great leaders face their fear and grow through it, give through it, and praise through it. Keep reading and learn how to harness a most powerful leadership tool: the human voice.

6 VOICE

V oice is the workhorse of leadership. Most of an active leader's day is spent in oral communication. Even mundane communication takes a special meaning when it comes from the leader. Whether persuading, motivating, or encouraging, leaders are constantly using their voice. What you say and how you say it makes a big difference. Generally, a leader's inability to communicate effectively foreshadows difficulties.

Have you ever attended a meeting filled with healthy discussion? People are talking up a storm. There are the loud talkers, proud talkers, and even disavowed talkers. When one person stops talking, another starts immediately. You patiently wait for your opportunity to speak. You have an idea, a good idea, and want desperately to share it, but you wait in silence. All the while, the gremlins of fear whisper persuasively in your ear: "Don't say anything! You will embarrass yourself! Your voice will be rejected and condemned! Forget that worthless idea of yours and say nothing!" Before you know it, the meeting is dismissed. Your idea is gone, and your voice was absent—missing in action.

Many of us hesitate to speak in public. While our ideas may be active and fertile, we lack confidence in speaking up. If you have trouble speaking in groups, you are not alone. Jesus once healed a man in Decapolis who was deaf and had trouble speaking. Jesus proclaimed, "Ephaphatha—be opened," and the man began to "speak plainly." The once uneasy speaker made the crowds marvel (Mark 7:34, NIV).

When the pressure is on, plain speech can feel like a heavenly event! This chapter will help you find your leadership voice. I address both the mindset (attitude) and technique of speaking well. Your voice shapes how others think and feel about you as a leader. Your influence is derived more from how you sound (vocal impact) and how you look (visual impact) than from the content of your words. [58] Yes, your body speaks, and your voice moves. When you lift your voice—in the right way, at the right time—you boost your visibility, connection, and influence as a leader.

If your voice is missing in action, so is your valuable input and contribution. Voice is the gatekeeper of influence. Name an influential leader—imagine an admired coach, teacher, CEO, pastor, or politician—and I bet you know and respect their voice. That person influences you because their voice makes you think, feel, and take action. Generally, if you do not like the leader's voice, you do not like the leader.

Employers of all stripes list verbal and written communication skills as critical to success in virtually all industries.[59] Whether you are speaking one-on-one or to thousands, finding your voice as a leader requires you to connect authentically, overcome fear, and release your best self.

Voice of Connection

The voice of the leader must be the language of the people. Your voice may be reasoned and intelligent, but if it does not connect, you are in serious trouble. When leaders focus only on what they want others to know, their message is bound to fail. A self-directed speech is a selfish speech; it drops faster than water rolling down a raincoat.

Effective speech is a two-way street, a dynamic exchange of ideas and information. Smart speakers create connection by focusing on the felt needs and wants of the audience. I ask myself three crucial questions to create audience connection:

- "What is the audience perspective?"

- "What do they really want to hear from me now?"

- "What is the audience ready to understand and absorb?"

Be sensitive to how your voice opens or closes the audience. Deliver your message only after you have established the attention and interest of your audience.

We are wired as humans to connect, and the voice of leadership is the glue that connects like-minded followers. Thousands of years ago, we lived as hunters and gathers in tribal enclaves of 20 to 150 people. The call of the leader was the rallying point for community life. When the leader's voice rang, it was the single most important happening of the day, setting the tone for community activity. If you wanted to eat, you listened for the call of the leader. If you wanted protection, you listened for the call of the leader. If you wanted vital information, you listened for the call of the leader. The call of the leader alerted followers to wake up, look out, and watch out. Ignore the call of the leader at your own peril.

We instinctively listen for the authentic, clarion call of a leader. The masses of people are waiting for the next leader. Many search endlessly for the leader to fulfill their hopes and desires. When a leader's message resonates, the audience will trust and follow. "I neither started the protest nor suggested it. I simply responded to the call of the people for a spokesman," said Dr. Martin Luther King Jr.[60] The right man or woman seems to rise at the right time.

Voice reflects deep emotions and feelings that move the spirit. We do not just listen to a voice; we feel it, we experience it, and we savor it. In fact, vocal tone is so powerful it can overshadow message content. Voice is like a powerful iceberg. The content of the words reflects the 10 percent of an iceberg visible from the surface. The emotional power comes from the 90 percent growing deep and wide below the surface of the water. Mobilize the full mass and power of your voice to have a lasting impact.

Public Voice

Say the word "speech," and most of us say, "No way!" When we see accomplished politicians, celebrities, and business leaders speak, we wonder how they do it. "I could never do that" is a common sentiment. After all, great speakers make it look natural. Yet the truth is that many of the most eloquent public leaders have spent decades refining their public voice. They learn through coaching, practice, and experience. They know skillful public speaking is a high-speed elevator that can quickly lift their leadership to the highest levels.

Leaders give voice to the voiceless. They know that the immediacy of a speech can galvanize support like nothing else. A speech can save a life, renew a life, and transform a life. It can make the audience wake up, stand up, and speak up. "As long as there are human rights to be defended; as long as there are great interests to be guarded; as long as the welfare of nations is a matter for discussion, so long will public speaking have its place," said William Jennings Bryan.[61]

Many leaders overestimate their ability to speak in public. They stand stiffer than a cardboard box. They stammer, hesitate, and dither their way through a speech. They say, "You know," twenty times a minute. The speech roams and rambles more than a preschool treasure hunt. The result is sanitized corporate communications more boring than a whitewashed tomb.

As a past president of Toastmasters International, I have seen hundreds of leaders rise to become effective public speakers. When you can express your ideas with polish and panache, promotion is predictable. Public speaking—the "leadership elevator"—is exciting to ride, but it can be a perilous journey. A public speech magnifies your persona. If you are serious about leadership, it is worth diligent effort.

In fact, public speaking is the purest form of your leadership brand. Your ideas can be stolen, your technology copied, and your staff recruited away, but there is one thing that your competition can *never* duplicate: your unique ability to communicate and connect with others. This is your leadership signature. It is the "you" in "your" brand. The written word can be edited to obscure errors and imperfections, but public speaking leaves no place to hide: The speaking style of the leader—reflected in examples, emotions, and word choices—gives a revealing glimpse of the leader's inner world, especially if the speech is extemporaneous. Good leaders use each speech to achieve a strategic purpose, seeding credibility and trust, which sprout persuasion and influence.

Publilius said, "Speech is the mirror of the soul; as a man speaks, so he is."[62] Voice is the clearest, most intimate medium of communication. More than brilliance or oratorical skill, voice links person to person, heart to heart, and spirit to spirit. And the style of the leader makes their voice endearing or irritating.

Story Voice

Leaders shape the reality to come with a story. We all have adventures and challenges in life. Framing is the ability to examine life experiences from multiple perspectives that serve a leadership objective. Whatever the topic, audiences love leaders who personalize their content in a story, teaching, humanizing, and inspiring. A strategic story positions the leader, providing a forward-leaning vision and a pathway to achieve it. A moving personal story can build an emotional connection with and devotion to the leader. Think of the keynote speech delivered at the Democratic National Convention in August 2004 by a little known Illinois state senator named Barack Obama. Yes, an eloquent, poignant story boosts your leadership brand.

I have shared my personal story hundreds of times. I was a shy senior at the University of California, Berkeley, looking forward to my graduation in the spring of 1985. I scheduled a final meeting with my faculty advisor, Dr. Milos Milutin Martic, to discuss my future. Dr. Martic was a beloved Berkeley professor who had immigrated from Yugoslavia in 1955 to found the political economy major within the International and Area Studies Program. "Your ideas are good, Michael, but you need to speak better … Find a way to speak better!" he admonished in his broken Yugoslavian accent.

Walking home after the meeting, I noticed a flyer posted on a campus billboard: "Join Toastmasters, Stand Up and Speak Out!" A stick figure displayed a confident speaking pose. *What is Toastmasters?* I wondered. Still pondering Dr. Martic's thoughtful counsel, I became interested in how Toastmasters could improve my speaking skills, so I kept reading. The flyer provided the meeting date, time, and location; I took a chance and attended the CAL Toastmasters Club, which met on Thursday evenings at the business school.

I joined CAL Toastmasters with high hopes. I wanted to learn to speak on my feet without falling on my face. One bad habit needed to change: When I stood up, my brain sat down. I intended to join for a few months and learn valuable speaking skills. When I spoke, however, on the challenges of growing up in a single-parent home, leaving Chicago for Berkeley, and playing on the CAL water polo team, I found my voice and connected with my audience. To my amazement, my personal story inspired others in unexpected ways. I started using personal anecdotes to reveal leadership wisdom, and after three decades as a Toastmasters leader, I am still doing it.

I quickly learned the power of story. If you are serious about leadership, you need to tell personal stories to make a point—a strategic story. Your story can crystallize your vision and motivate others to follow you. It is the surest way to put a human face on trials and tragedies. Perhaps you are asking, "Why would anyone want to hear my story?" Your story makes your life—with all its failures and successes—

understandable and accessible. Here are a few reasons leaders need to tell stories:

- **A Story Educates**: Stories are open, metaphorical constructs that illuminate human strengths and foibles. They help us process and remember information. When boring data is placed in the context of a story, it suddenly comes alive. Knowledge is reshaped into something meaningful, which is easily transmitted to others. I am fifty-five years old as I write this chapter. Learning everything from personal experience would take me many lifetimes, but a well-placed story provides helpful guidance for life's journey.

- **A Story Inspires**: A story aptly spoken heals a heart badly broken. The right story spoken at the right time brings renewal, optimism, and hope. Somebody in the audience needs to hear your story. When you have the courage to share an authentic story, it gives others the hope to believe that what you have done is possible for them.

- **A Story Sells**: Your story "sells" your brand to the world. Like it or not, we are all in the selling business. If we do not sell a product, we sell our ideas, hopes, and ambitions. When the audience relates to your story, they relate to you and the ideas you sell. Abstract ideas become relevant and meaningful when illustrated through the power of a story.

- **A Story Distinguishes**: A story makes you unique and distinguishes you from your competition. You are no longer just a face in the crowd. The audience gains insights into what you strive for and value in life. A well-positioned story recreates life meaning and relevance, allowing others to draw wisdom from your experience.

- **A Story Unites**: Our culture creates status lines based on appearance, education, wealth, and status. Leaders are often placed on a pedestal. But a story levels the speaker with the audience. As Toastmasters president, I told my story and instantly united with the audience.

Leaders stay close to their calling by staying close to their stories. When you share a relevant, poignant story, you have the potential to interrupt an audience member's internal dialogue. Your story can help followers think differently about themselves, the organization, and your leadership.

Stories find you when you least expect it. Be on the lookout for good stories to illustrate your message. A story that moves you is likely to move others. Sometimes, the most inspiring stories arise from the darkest experiences. An uncomfortable story is the one others most need to hear. When you are washed up on a rocky shoreline, look for the shells with the beautiful pearls within.

Never discount your own story. You do not need to be a valedictorian, star athlete, military hero, or recovering heroin addict to tell an engaging story. Most people do not relate to these spectacular examples anyway. Most of us lead average lives with hidden nuggets of wisdom waiting to be discovered.

The key to telling your story, and telling it well, is to speak with an authentic and audience-centered voice. Your story voice comes from the heart. If possible, avoid reading from a script. Be expressive and natural. Practice your delivery. Then record yourself, replay it, and notice the areas that need improvement. Refine your story through the use of a clear voice, concise voice, and confident voice:

- **Clear Voice**: Speak loudly with active verbs, short direct sentences, and clear annunciation. Repeat key words and phrases to help audience retention. Avoid excessive alcohol before speaking. Never leave the audience confused over what is wanted or needed. Provide others with a simple, clear path. The clear voice helps others plainly see, feel, and experience your desired outcomes.

- **Concise Voice**: Articulate brevity is speaking mastery. In an era of information overload, the concise voice is rare and treasured. Learn to say no more than what is necessary. If you fall in love with your own speaking voice, break it off before the marriage. In my over three decades as a speaker, I have never heard an audience complain about a speaker who is too brief. My motto is simple: Always stop speaking before the audience wishes I would. In the words of Franklin D. Roosevelt, "Be sincere, be brief and be seated."[63]

- **Confident Voice**: Confidence comes from attitude and preparation. Create a message you believe with all your heart and rehearse it out loud. Become comfortable with the microphone, room, and audience. Stand tall, breathe deep, and speak from your chest, radiating gratitude and optimism. Find a comfortable speaking rate that allows the audience time to absorb your ideas, but not time to wander. Pause after important words and phrases. Avoid distracting filler words like "you know" and "aah," and avoid improvised digressions. Focus your mental energy outward toward connecting and giving to the audience.

Anxious Voice

I wish I was better at taking my own advice on public speaking. As a top-producing commercial real estate broker, I earned an invitation to speak at a prestigious luncheon meeting of commercial real estate professionals at the elegant Hyatt Regency Hotel in downtown San Francisco, California. I was thirty-one years old. My career was surging! It was my chance to shine as a speaker, build my professional brand, and demonstrate leadership in the Bay Area commercial real estate community. I was excited!

After weeks of preparation and anticipation, the big day came. I prepared a speech long on impressive statistics and market data, but short on personal stories. I arrived early at the speaking venue to greet people as they arrived in the elegant hotel ballroom. The meeting was called to order at noon. I sat on an ornate dais in my best suit and talked with the meeting organizers while lunch was served. As the lunch plates cleared, the master of ceremonies gave me a nice introduction. I proudly strutted to the lectern, adjusted the microphone, and looked out at an audience of *big eyes* and *power ties*. Suddenly, my heart started pounding like a jackhammer. My thoughts began racing on the NASCAR circuit. My mouth became a dry and parched desert. My legs were shaking and quaking. My sweaty palms were as cold as shivering ice cycles. My brain was a train pulling out of the station with nothing attached. I wanted to get the speech over, so I spoke a little faster … and a little faster … and a little faster. When it was over, I delivered a twenty-five-minute speech in ten minutes. I spoke so quickly, my tongue got a speeding ticket!

After the speech, I stood at the door and watched as 250 professionals walked out of the ballroom in silence. Nobody made eye contact with me. Nobody said a word. When I got back to my office, I called a friend who had been in the audience and asked him what he thought. "It was a disaster, Michael, a disaster … an absolute disaster," he said.

I then called a trusted client who had been in the audience, expecting a comforting word. But he refused to take my call, and we have never spoken since. How bad could it have been? I estimate that I lost over a half-million dollars in potential commercial real estate commissions from one poorly delivered speech. I would have done better financially to burn my house down!

That speech was delivered in 1993. It turned over a new chapter in my life. Failure motivated me to improve my public speaking skills. At the time, I was a novice Toastmaster who avoided consistent public speaking practice. I believed I was *already* a capable and competent public speaker, so I approached Toastmasters cavalierly. How wrong I was. I soon recognized there is big difference between speaking to 20 people and 200. My skills wavered as the audience grew. Yes, a great speech can lift you to success, but a bad speech can drop you faster than a lead balloon. A silver tongue can enhance your reputation, but a tied tongue can unravel it just as quickly.

"There are two types of speakers in the world: the nervous and liars," said Mark Twain.[64] Most of us experience some level of fear and anxiety when speaking in public. Fear drives the body's ancient fight-or-flight response, and rational thought is lost. At birth, we have only two fears: the fear of falling and the fear of loud noises.[65] Every other fear is a learned reaction.

If you do not feel some nervousness, you are probably not human. From modest nerves to panic attacks, public speaking can become uncomfortable or even debilitating. Only when we face our fear can we conquer it. Denial grows fear. Understanding the triggers that create fear of public speaking can help us replace fear with confidence.

Fear can freeze your nerves and ruin your speech. My friend Toastmaster Don Ensch watched a terrified speaker pass out while giving a speech at the Sandpiper

Toastmaster Club in Ventura, California. Even the most successful speakers experience some level of anxiety before presenting. Fear is hard to eliminate entirely. When you recognize the cause of your fear, you can do something about it. Here are four fears that form the root cause for the fear of public speaking:

- **Fear of Looking Foolish**: Blind spots, mistakes, and blemishes get amplified on the speaker's stage. The prospect of saying or doing something incorrect, inappropriate, or embarrassing can ruin your fun. Remedy: Maintain a prespeaking checklist for rehearsal, fact-checking, dress, and appearance.

- **Fear of Feeling Uncomfortable**: Public speaking creates an altered physiological state. Your pulse quickens, throat tightens, mouth dries, and ideas race. Some speakers become stiff and frozen, which makes them painful to watch. Remedy: Practice light exercise, stretching, self-massage, deep breathing, or humming a favorite song. Anything to help you feel good—but avoid alcohol or drugs (unless prescribed by a doctor).

- **Fear of Loss of Control**: Public speaking is a wildcard, even under the best circumstances. Nobody can totally control what happens on stage or in the audience. Between interruptions, fire alarms, power outages, and sound failures, the speaker needs to be ready for anything. Remedy: Relish the challenge of meeting unexpected challenges.

- **Fear of Being Alone**: The speaking spotlight can be a lonely place. We are by nature social animals and seek community connection. Standing apart to deliver a speech pulls us away from our natural community. Remedy: Show up early and make friends in the audience. Visualize yourself supporting the audience from the front.

Left unattended, the fear of public speaking can become a roaring dragon, spewing damaging and judgmental self-talk. Great communicators take control of their fears through preparation and practice. I encourage new speakers to have fun and go easy on themselves. Adopt the attitude that each speech is a love gift to the audience. The same adrenaline rush that terrifies can release energy, enthusiasm, and charisma. Overcome fear through energizing your delivery, reframing speaking anxiety into positive expectation and performance energy.

High-visibility speeches can increase nervousness if the speaker holds unreasonable personal expectations. When you think, *I must make the sale*, or, *I must impress this audience*, anxiety grows. What speaker can really control audience reaction? Even the best speakers occasionally receive a weak response. For the nervous speaker, the difference between achievable and unreasonable expectations causes fear to grow. Recover peace of mind and control by affirming the speaker's bill of rights:

- "I can deliver a great speech even if some audience members do not like me."

- "I can deliver a great speech even if some audience members do not fully understand me."

- "I can deliver a great speech even if some audience members do not believe and trust me."

This does not diminish the importance of engaging and impacting your audience. But it gives the speaker the freedom to silence the inner critic, speak passionately, and not be inhibited by self- judgment. While a public speech is not right for every occasion, it can unify a team, underscore your values, and steer the audience toward success. Yes, a well-tuned speech can make a big difference.

And never forget the important role of humor in diminishing fear. I once gave a speech challenging an eager audience to confront the fear of public speaking. "Your fears do not serve you; they stifle you!" I proclaimed. "Most of what you fear never happens. FEAR is an acronym for False Expectations Appearing Real."

A man in the audience jumped up and said, "You are crazy. FEAR stands for Forget Everything And Run." Then he ran out of the room!

The King's Voice

The award-winning film The King's Speech is a testament to the transformational power of a leader who found his voice. Prince Albert (played by actor Colin Firth) is the Duke of York, the second son of George V and second in line to become the king of England. But Albert has a stuttering problem that makes his public speaking agonizing. Destined to become King George VI when his elder brother abdicates the throne, Prince Albert seeks professional help for his problem.

First, he tries the traditional methods, which seem to make matters worse. He then engages an avant-garde speech therapist named Lionel Logue (played by Geoffrey Rush) to help him overcome his stuttering. Logue builds a warm and endearing friendship with the future king as he guides Prince Albert in vocal exercises, muscle relaxation, and breath control. Logue's personal relationship with Prince Albert helps him address the psychological reasons for his speech impairment.

The hard work of the two men pays off handsomely. Logue is instrumental in helping the new king deliver his first wartime speech, which is a resounding success. In one signature exchange, a dejected and stuttering Prince Albert says, "I can't be the king."

Logue retorts, "Yes, you can be a great king!"

In Logue, Prince Albert found more than a coach and mentor; he found a friend. The affable, warm relationship contrasted with the stiff formality of his royal position. The collaborative synergy between the two men transformed the future king. Albert moved from feckless to fearless, from panic to power. The courage of a leader is contagious. The personal pluck of King George VI provides an inspiring example for speakers of all stripes.

Public speaking is a skill that will improve with practice. Effective leaders create a conversation with their audience—whether an audience of 1 or 1,000. Audience members feel you are speaking directly to them. Connection is the breakthrough flash, the epiphany moment. When the speaker and audience start thinking together, moving together, and feeling together, anything is possible. Like a graceful ballroom dancer, the speaker and audience become one in spirit. While the audience may forget what you said, they never forget the way you made them feel. Watch the body cues in the audience to see if your talk is connecting. Do you see smiles and appreciation or frowns and fidgeting? Do you feel absorption or apathy? Eloquence is the voice of connected wisdom.

Good public speaking has a natural, extemporaneous quality. Helpful ideas are transmitted naturally with action and immediacy. Gliding on the winsome words of a leader, doors open and hearts are won. As Prince Albert discovered in *The King's Speech*, public speaking is a skill that requires practice and patience. It does not happen overnight, and the road to mastery is filled with discovery and personal growth. Do it well and you control your leadership destiny.

Release Your Voice

Whether you are a prince or pauper, some anxiety is part of public speaking, and most of us hide tension in our vocal chords. Tense speakers create a high-pitched, stretched sound, causing the voice to fade and quiver. The result is a screechy, whiney sound. Vocal tension makes you feel like a tightly twisted wet rag waiting for something to come out. Working with emerging leaders, I have developed a set of vocal exercises to help release vocal tension and warm up your vocal chords for speaking:

- **YALE** (the Yawn And Laugh Exercise): Begin by massaging your jaws. Then roll your neck. Vocalize a big yawn while opening your jaws. Slowly let the yawn transition into a laugh. Give out a hearty belly laugh. Feel your throat and neck opening, and your vocal chords relaxing. YALE is a great performance enhancer if you feel you need a little pep before delivering a speech.

- **Panting**: Open your mouth and begin to pant like a dog. Focus on projecting air as far as it will go. Slowly stick out your tongue as you continue to pant air forward. This is also a great way to prepare for projecting your voice.

- **Lip Drill**: This exercise will help your articulators. Press your finger on your cheeks and press air through your mouth while vibrating your lips. You should sound like a big propeller.

- **Aye, Aye, Aye**: Imagine that you are in the navy and repeat, "Aye, aye, aye," moving through higher and lower octaves. As you say, "Aye," practice modulating your voice through moving your tongue in parallel. As your tongue moves up and down, say, "Aye, aye, aye." This is a great warm-up to feel your vocal range.

Why pay all this attention to the sound of your voice? Voice is your leadership calling card. Vocal exercises help the speaker relax, lower pitch, and project energy outward. With infinite potential for inflection, nuance, and emphasis, the human voice is a powerful and precious instrument. Voice radiates what a person is feeling, whether good or bad. Think of the last time you spoke with a friend on the phone. Instantly, the voice tells you the mood of the speaker. The content of the words is almost secondary. The real story is in the pitch and emphasis of the voice.

Many leaders have only one color in their vocal range. They speak in a monotone, to the disappointment of enduring ears. Others only add emotional color to their voice when they are upset, frustrated, or angry. I once coached a leader who insisted the sound of his voice did not really matter because he spoke "just the facts." As he explained, "I do it one way, my way, which is the best way." This is a wrong mindset. Your voice is never neutral. It is *always* advancing or diminishing you as the leader.

The human ear abhors sameness and monotony. A monotonous sound puts many of us to sleep. Think of the professor who reads the textbook during a lecture—and puts the students to sleep. Variety perks our attention and keeps us wondering what is going to happen next. When sounds are changing, we naturally perk up and pay attention.

A limited vocal range narrows the speaker's interest, appeal and connection with the audience. Imagine an artist preparing to paint a beautiful backyard garden. Plants of every color dot the terrain, including red roses, blue tangos, white carnations, pink geraniums, orange tiger flowers, and yellow begonias. But the artist has only one paint color: beige. Beige is great for painting potatoes, but quite dreary for painting a colorful garden. When you speak in a monotone, you paint your speech tone in one lifeless color.

Here are ways to add variety and color to your voice:

- **Volume**: The most important rule of speaking is to be audible. All audience members need to hear you, no matter their age. Your voice volume should vary, ranging from soft to loud. Avoid shouting or whispering, except briefly. As a baseline, be loud enough for others to hear but not so loud that you overpower the audience. If speaking to a large group, use a microphone whenever possible and raise your volume when moving toward a climax. When the volume shifts, the audience will associate a mood shift. For instance, a strong, confident speaker who suddenly becomes soft and intimate arouses attention. Studies show that volume variation creates power and authority.[66]

- **Pitch**: Minute fluctuations in air pressure flowing through the vocal tract produce variations in pitch. Each of us has a natural pitch range, and women tend to have a higher pitch range than men. Imagine the longer, thicker strings on a guitar, which vibrate with a lower pitch. Our voices fluctuate in much the same way. While leaders with lower-pitched voices are deemed more authoritative, all speakers should modulate through their natural pitch range to achieve a positive impact. Finding your leadership voice can take many years. Research by UCLA acoustic scientist Rosario Signorello revealed charismatic leaders drop their vocal tone for greater authority and lift their vocal pitch to show passion.[67] Confident leaders project positive self-esteem, which tells the world we can overcome any obstacle. We associate a deeper vocal tone with confidence. Within a world of nattering nabobs of negativism, the self-confident leader stands out.

- **Tempo**: Tempo is speaking rate. Talk too quickly and you overwhelm your audience. Talk too slowly and people go to sleep. Find a natural speaking rate by engaging in natural conversation with a friend, taping it, and counting your speaking rate. For most of us, that rate is in the range of 130 to 165 words per minute. Increase speed to enhance content energy; lower speed to enhance understanding and emotional impact.

- **Silence**: The most underappreciated vocal tool is the pause. Silence is golden in speaking. In fact, more is said between the words. When the audience has time to let the ideas land, the full impact of the communication is realized. If you are a fast speaker, like me, the best advice is to script pauses into your speaking. This gives others time to think and absorb what you say. The rate is slow and rhythmic, leaving plenty of strategic pauses to absorb the message.

- **Timbre**: Timbre reflects the emotional color of your voice. Are you happy? Are you sad? Timbre radiates the attitude, inflection, and emphasis of the speaker's emotions. Speech is built on timbre distinctions. Timbre is often detected through the resonance of the voice. The audience can tell when the speaker is caring and committed. If there is dissonance between the content of the message (happy), but the vocal timber is sad, the audience will distrust the speaker.

Like a sunken treasure, your golden speaking voice is waiting to be revealed and released. You will discover a most appealing, sonorous, and persuasive voice. Experiment with vocal variation. Go high and low, fast and slow, smooth and jagged. Try going all-out, then pull it back and find a comfortable, warm sweet spot that works for you. Dynamics in tone, volume, pitch, and body movement make the speaker more engaging and interesting. A variable delivery keeps the audience always watching and listening in suspense.

Let go of the stiffness. A dynamic delivery should flow naturally from the release of your energy and vitality for the topic. In contrast, a monotone destroys the appeal of the speaker. We live in a world of constant change. In the electronic age, the attention span of your audience is as long as it takes them to pop out their smartphone and check text messages. Choose topics that excite you and you will excite your audience. A speaker lacking dynamics will put you to sleep. Get out from behind the lectern. Move and gesture freely.

An optimum speaking rate of approximately 150 words per minute gives an average audience adequate comprehension time. Project your energy outward through your voice. Confident speakers skillfully modulate emphasis, inflection, and intonation while speaking. Low-energy speakers lack variation and speak with a monotone. When the words have no energy, the impact is diminished. Power comes from varying volume, pitch, and rate.

Effective leaders manage their voice. They become skilled at shaping communication to maximize impact. How do you start? By listening to a recording of your own voice on your smartphone voice recorder. Why? While you hear your voice every day, hearing sound through your head is different from what your audience hears. Record and read a simple text in your natural tone. Then listen to yourself. "Is that really me?" is a common response. "Do I really sound like that?" Yes, the recording is exactly what your audience hears. Is this the voice of leadership? Would I follow my voice if I had the opportunity?

Your voice is a magical instrument that can captivate, elevate, or devastate. The voice of leadership is a deep, authoritative, and resonant. This does not mean all of us need to sound like John Paul Jones or Charlton Heston. It does mean that a high, nasal-sounding voice diminishes your leadership potential. Most people can bring their voice to a deeper register that projects authority and confidence.

If you decide to give a public speech, resolve to do it well. Dedicating the time and resources to speaking well pays rich personal and professional dividends. Public speaking is a tool to highlight your values, magnify your vision, and build your brand. Like a bowl of Rice Krispies, a good speech should snap, crackle, and pop. The introduction snaps the audience to attention, the body crackles with meaningful content, and the conclusion pops the audience to take action.

Summary

Leadership is finding your voice and using it to impact the world. The voice of the leader must be clearly understood. While our world is filled with plenty of empty talk, real communication is a two-way exchange that changes both the speaker and listener.

Public speaking is rarely a natural skill. It takes practice. If you expect to grow as a leader, but fail to develop your communication skills, your advancement will be impeded. Not all speakers are leaders, but all effective leaders communicate clearly, confidently, and concisely. Poor communication skills are like a leaky garden bucket, sprouting weeds of suspicion and mistrust.

Leaders elevate their brand quickly through effective public speaking. Your personal speaking style—reflected in examples, emotions, and word choices—gives the audience a revealing glimpse of your inner world. Use public speaking to achieve a strategic purpose, seeding credibility and trust, which sprout persuasion and influence. Strategic stories make the speaker believable. Leaders use stories to educate, inspire, sell, distinguish, and unite.

Fear is a common impediment to effective public speaking. Do you fear looking foolish, feeling uncomfortable, losing control, or being alone on stage? Overcome the dread of public speaking by isolating and eliminating your source of fear.

Rampant fear can make public speaking unpleasant and embarrassing. But fear can be overcome through preparation, practice, and humor. Learn to have fun and imagine each speech as a love gift to the audience. The same adrenaline rush that terrifies can release energy, enthusiasm, and charisma. Practice speaking with an energized delivery that transforms anxiety into positive performance energy. Remember the speaker's bill of rights: It is impossible to please everybody all the time—so don't try!

Voice is your golden nugget. Practice vocal exercises to release tension and add vocal variety by varying volume, pitch, tempo, silence, and timbre. Develop a dynamic vocal range that keeps your audience alert and attentive.

The call of the leader is finding your voice—the authentic, credible message that builds trust and invites commitment—and telling your story in an interesting, compelling way.

When you find it, others know it, you know it, and the world stands up and takes note. The more personal your voice, the more powerful your impact. Voice is a powerful medium to achieve the objective of our next chapter: building the rhythm of success.

Chapter 7

RHYTHM

ike the beat of a favorite song, your calling provides a constant source of forward momentum and energy. The rhythm of the leader quickens the collaborative spirit and positions team members for success. Followers draw on the tempo of the leader to shape work cadence and capacity. When the rhythm is robust and healthy, supporters accept high standards and increased levels of responsibility and accountability.

Rhythm is the magic behind culture, and culture shapes everything you do as a leader. Many leaders mistakenly believe that culture is intangible and unchangeable. When challenges rise, they cast structural changes from the top, ignoring the human rhythm of the organization. Rhythm cuts to the heartbeat of a group, reforming ethics, values, and communication patterns while reshaping work habits. If a leader attempts change without addressing rhythm, they often cause cosmetic changes that ignore underlying problems.

The toughest part of creating a successful rhythm is getting started. Motion begets motion. A parked car goes no place, but when it moves, it is easy to steer. It is time to get the rhythm flowing!

The Rhythm of Yes

Yes is the rhythm of champions. Leaders find a way to say yes when they can. Yes is the conduit that open doors and makes beautiful results possible. "If someone offers you an amazing opportunity and you are not sure you can do it, say yes. Then learn how to do it later," said Sir Richard Branson.[68] Leaders capitalize on the breaks and opportunities that come their way.

Yes is an exciting journey. Yes affirms the confidence others have in you. You take a leap of faith and discover your wings on the way down. Often, we allow fears to pull us away from life's brilliant opportunities. When opportunity knocks, don't complain about the noise. Be thankful; the lucky break may never come again. Leaders find a way to say yes to good ideas, regardless of their source.

I enjoy improvisation classes. Improv adopts the mindset of saying, "Yes and ...," to all offers and invitations whenever possible. For example, if a performer hands you an imaginary fish on stage, you might say, "Yes, and you, sir, are a fine fisherman!" The act of affirming your partner and taking it one step further builds the dialogue while creating connection, fun, and spontaneity. The power of yes empowers everyone in the scene to do their best. My first improvisation class was rather clumsy and mechanical. Soon, I got the hang of giving offers and receiving offers with yes, yes, yes.

In contrast, saying no closes opportunities that are lost forever. In the early 1970s, my father had the good fortune of sitting alongside one of Ray Kroc's top executives from McDonald's Corporation on a long flight from Los Angeles to Chicago. The two men got along famously. At the time, McDonald's was an emerging franchise operation with unknown potential. The executive offered my dad a ground-floor opportunity to purchase multiple McDonald's franchises for a pittance. "Will you purchase a franchise, Mr. Notaro?"

"No, no, no," my father replied. "There is no long-term potential in fast food; food is a common commodity, and fast food is a fad destined to fail." My father spent weeks marching around the house justifying his "no." If only he had said yes!

Searching for a reason to say yes is listening for the call of the leader. "No" is painfully obvious. It is the louder, boisterous voice. Of course, saying no is appropriate for anything illegal, immoral, and imprudent. But saying no because it is convenient is a form of personal denial. In contrast, "yes" is the potential stirring within your soul. Will you listen? Take time to absorb the resonant spirit of "yes" within. It will change your life.

For many years, my natural inclination was to say no to new opportunities. It saved me the fear of the unknown and made the request go away. But that changed when I joined Toastmasters International. Instead of closing to new opportunities, I welcomed them. When invited to speak, I said yes. The more I said yes, the more invitations I received. Soon, I was speaking to businesses, nonprofits, and community groups. I was addicted to saying yes and became a yes-a-holic. The police could have pulled me over for excessive speaking. The rhythm of yes opened new opportunities for personal growth, fun, and leadership development.

Rhythm and Harmony

When people say yes together, they create a collective spirit of harmony. Ordinary people saying yes can achieve extraordinary results. The unifying chorus creates harmony, a consistent, orderly arrangement of parts. The word harmony is from the Greek word harmonia, which means "joint agreement,"[69] and the word harmozo, which means "to fit together, to join."[70] The rhythm of success is the joint agreement to grow, stretch, and achieve together. In a self-centered, self-seeking, self-interested world, this can be a difficult challenge for the leader. People do not naturally work together in harmony.

I learned the value of cadence as a sophomore in high school when I joined the crew team. Crew is the ultimate team and rhythm sport. The shell (boat) has a crew of eight oarsmen and a coxswain, who shouts instructional commands. Timing and synchronous movement are crucial to success. Regardless of individual strengths, if the crew fails to catch, pull, and recover oars in harmony together, the boat rocks, sways, and slows.

Many strong athletes fail at crew because they cannot pull and recover in harmony with the other oarsmen. Crew is not for anyone who wants to be an individual star. Drawing personal attention often disrupts team chemistry, slowing the boat. For the crew to succeed, every oarsman must be the MVP. When oarsmen match bladework in perfect harmony, the shell moves faster with less effort. Winning teammates excel with powerful harmony.

The leader of the boat is the coxswain. The coxswain is the voice of teamwork; shouting instructions to a crew is commonly known as "calling." Calls such as "Weigh up," "Touch up," and "Square up" provide guidance for clear changes in behavior. Commands need to be clear and simple, because the crew is focused on rowing, not interpreting. Commands called with a consistent, positive cadence inspire the crew. The first command notifies the crew of a change, the second counts down the change, and the third executes the change. Effective race strategy includes a coxswain calling the start, calling for "Power 10" (i.e., timed exertion), and calling for the sprint. There is no simple way to make the boat move faster. Each crew has its own personality and responds differently. What works in one crew may cause problems in another.

To the casual observer, a skilled crew elegantly moves across the water, gliding like a beautiful swan. Do not be fooled—crew is a grueling sport. Rowers are some of the best-conditioned athletes in the world. The sport involves all major muscle groups and demands balance, strength, mental discipline, and an acute sense of timing.

How can a crew maximize speed and efficiency? Good coxswains read their crew and establish the optimum rowing cadence. The cadence should reinforce proper technique, timing, and teamwork to move the boat forward smoothly. Execute a stroke count that is too high and the crew fatigues quickly. Execute a stroke count that is too slow and the shell moves slower than it should. The coxswain balances the need to get ahead early with the need to save energy for a strong finish. If you exhaust the crew early, they will have nothing for the final sprint.

The rower in the stroke position sits closest to the coxswain and sets the rhythm of the boat for the rest of the rowers. This is position number eight, farthest from the front. Our coach was Mr. Swift. We had shirts printed up that said "Swifty," and most of the time that is how we rowed. I was assigned to the front of the boat, the bow, known as position number one. This is the part of the boat that crosses the finish line first. From the front looking backward, I could see the other seven rowers and the coxswain.

My most memorable race came against St. Paul's Academy in Concord, New Hampshire. We started at a high stroke rate, but we were still tied at the halfway point. The coxswain dropped our rate while the other team maintained a high stroke count and surged. Toward the end, St. Paul started sprinting but had nothing left. We waited to sprint and had something left. Timing is everything in crew and leadership.

Successful leaders adjust the rhythm to maximize the performance of the team. Knowing when to increase the stroke count is crucial to success. Demanding higher stroke rates does not always result in greater speed. A technically talented crew that maintains efficiency and power may cover more water faster than a less-capable crew rowing a high stroke rate. Let team members establish a stroke rate that is right for them.

Leaders set the tempo and cadence for organizational success. Go too slow and the business loses money. Go too fast and you burn everyone out. What is the call of the leader in your organization? Are you moving in harmonious alignment? Are you racing or lagging? Are all of your team members pulling their weight? Your leadership brand resonates with a cadence that inspires or repels.

Changing the Rhythm

What is the winning stroke rate for your team? Leaders with a winning rhythm set an example that can be modeled and replicated by others. During my term as Toastmasters

International president, I visited a Toastmasters district inflamed with rancor and dissention. Within minutes of my arrival, the top leaders were arguing—drowning each other in a sea of insults. When they weren't openly quarreling, they gave each other the silent treatment. The mood was more toxic than a Chernobyl nuclear reactor. The fractious culture made me wonder why anybody would want to associate with them. One leader told me bluntly, "People keep their distance around here. You should do the same."

As international president, I knew I had to do something to change the toxic culture, but I didn't know where to start. There was plenty of blame to go around, and as just a weekend visitor, my knowledge of the symptoms was limited. Ordinarily, the visit of the international president brings local leaders together, who present their best face. In this district, the infighting was so great that nobody seemed to care. They appeared set on enduring the dignitary visit while minimizing public embarrassment.

I waited for the right opportunity to change the negative culture. It came before my keynote speech at the district conference on Saturday morning. I entered the assembly hall early to get ready for my speech and assess the audience. I saw somber faces and lonely stares. Over 200 people sat in dead silence in a large assembly hall. The human temperature was below freezing. Nobody said a word, an atmosphere very unusual for our organization. Toastmasters are talkers, and events are generally social and friendly. "Why is this room so quiet?" I asked a local leader.

"People do not have much to say to each other around here," she lamented.

I rose from my seat and started enthusiastically greeting the first row of the seated audience. "My name is Michael Notaro, and I am glad to meet you," I said. I spoke to each person individually and asked them about their experience as a Toastmaster. Five minutes later, I had worked my way through the first row. I noticed the entire room was staring at me in shock. The district leaders could not believe what was happening.

Then I moved back to the second row and continued greeting each person individually in sequence. While greeting, I could hear the people in the first row, who were continuing to talk to one another. I finished greeting the second row and moved to the third row, then continued methodically working seat by seat, row by row, through the entire audience. Most members were grateful to speak with me. I could feel the energy rising in the room. People were laughing and talking with one another. When I reached the back of the room, I realized it was a different audience. Now they were ready to hear a speech!

I walked back to my seat in the front. To my surprise, I saw a glorious sight: Each of the top three district leaders was following my lead, working through the audience seat by seat and row by row, greeting the Toastmasters. In an instant, the attitude had changed among the leaders. There was a new rhythm of success in the district. The district conference was highly successful, and the positive momentum helped change attitudes and inspire a successful year.

As leaders, actions speak louder than words. Values are more than platitudes posted on the company's website. They must be lived out each day by leaders. Be proactive creating the culture you desire. By taking charge of introductions, I was able to shift the mood and cause members to think differently. I could have given a speech on hospitality and kindness, but it would not have had the same powerful effect.

Leaders are the human thermostat. When the human temperature chills, the leader warms the room with infectious optimism. Connections increase as the temperature rises. And when the heat is overwhelming, leaders provide cooling refreshment.

Later that day, I gave a luncheon program. Before the event started, someone told me the conference chair was on the verge of a nervous breakdown. As I prepared for my speech, the facilities coordinator had asked if the conference chair had received my PowerPoint slides.

"What PowerPoint slides?" the conference chair had responded. "Does he want to use PowerPoint slides?" she recoiled. It was clear that she was at the breaking point, and she rushed out of the room.

A few minutes later, the distraught facilities chair reappeared and apologized. "I am sorry, so sorry, Michael, but we cannot do PowerPoint," she said with exasperation and embarrassment.

I think she expected me to erupt in anger with her announcement. "Not a problem. I have plenty of power in my points already. I will speak without slides."

I delivered my presentation without PowerPoint, and the audience did not know the difference. The conference chair relaxed when she realized the lack of powerpoint did nothing to diminish the conference. I maintained the rhythm of success despite an unplanned complication, and everyone was better for it.

Learning the Rhythm

Leaders find the winning rhythm, regardless of what's happening around them, and the rhythm supports the music. Leaders play the high notes, maintaining the sharps and avoiding the flats. Calling out the high notes keep others looking up, playing up, and living up to positive expectations.

The secret is learning to play the three As with poise and panache:

$$Attitude (A) + Aptitude (A) = Altitude(A)$$

- **Attitude**: Attitude is the inner feeling that shapes your outer reality. Zig Ziglar once said, "Your attitude, not your aptitude, determines your altitude."[71] A positive demeanor has a way of transcending education, appearance, and skill. Cheerful optimism radiates from facial expressions, body language, and vocal energy, attracting friends and supporters. We may tolerate the illogical, irrational, or nonsensical, but a toxic attitude spells immediate trouble. "I don't like that person's attitude" often precedes firing that person. In contrast, every team makes room for a sincere voice with a positive attitude.

- **Aptitude**: Aptitude is the skill set that shapes your professional competency. Are you fit to achieve your calling? Are you well-connected, well-read, and well-spoken? Make the pursuit of self-improvement a life habit. Build and refine your professional skills at every opportunity. Seek mentors, read books, attend seminars, and continuously improve your skills, and become a leader who radiates excellence in all you do.

- **Altitude**: Altitude is the height of your achievement. How high will your team rise? The rhythm of leadership lifts every team member to reach their full potential. Big people with big ideas produce big results. Team commitment to higher standards raises expectations and drives excellence. When a like-minded, capable team commits to high-altitude achievement, anything is possible.

Attitude is a choice. Aptitude is skill. Altitude is results. Attitude grows aptitude, which drives altitude. When a person has a good attitude, they are more likely to focus on career growth and team success. Like a favorite song, the leader plays the three As—attitude, aptitude, and altitude—every day and never skips a beat. The melodious rhythm of success shapes a winning culture for all to celebrate.

Holding the Rhythm

A positive attitude comes easy when times are good; the real challenge is maintaining a consistent positive attitude in hard times. Leaders get more than their fair share of setbacks and adversities. You cannot control what happens to you, but you can control how you respond to it. Response is a choice. You can choose an inner dialogue that empowers and motivates, or you can choose one that depresses and defeats.

A consistent positive attitude comes from self-discipline. The intention to think and act positively will set you apart from the masses, but it requires mobilizing the internal power of your calling. Find the resolve within—the calling power—to work hard even when you do not feel like it. As president of Toastmasters, I never got sick of speaking to new members, but I did feel my energy waning at times. When I considered that each new member contact could change a life (like it did for me), my attitude was renewed. Reflecting on my calling gave me the discipline to meet one more member and make one more appearance.

Lack of self-discipline is the stumbling block that tears down most leaders. If you had the discipline to do the hard things, think how much more successful you would be. Begin simply by establishing daily work habits that energize, motivate, and empower. Effective leaders rise early, exercise, find inspiration, and give and take loving support. "Good habits are worth being fanatical about," said John Irving.[72] The disciplines of the leader vary based on personal goals and objectives. You can take control of your destiny through rigorous success habits.

Focus on building your success rhythm by living with consistent values, a consistent work ethic, and consistent communications:

- **Consistent Values**: Values are more than noble statements on a website. They must be lived out in people on a daily basis, or they are nothing at all. If you claim to value fun, your actions must demonstrate fun. If you value innovation and creativity, team members need the freedom to pursue new strategies and ideas without criticism. If you value health but are hundreds of pounds overweight, credibility is lacking. Recognize that your values will be tested. If you abandon them at the first opportunity, they are not really values at all.

- **Consistent Work Ethic**: The rhythm of leadership goes hand in hand with a reliable, predictable work ethic. The leader needs to be dependable. Pay attention to details that create a positive example for others. Early is on time; on time is late; and late is a problem. When team members have a strong work ethic, they produce more with less and have greater levels of respect in themselves.

- **Consistent Communications**: Leadership communications should consistently inform, inspire, and educate. Whenever confusion reigns in an organization, there is a leader who is failing to communicate. Messaging should have a reliable, upbeat tone that pulls people together and pushes them forward. You may think you communicate too much. When you think followers are getting sick of hearing you, they are probably just beginning to listen. Positive truth expressed through positive communication creates positive results.

Great leadership is the rhythm of disciplined excellence. You pay it forward as the leader, modeling everything you want to see in followers. Holding the high notes takes persistence and practice. It always takes longer than expected, but eventually teammates will play up to your example. "People like consistency. Whether it is a store or restaurant, they want to come in and see what you are famous for," said Millard Drexler.[73]

The Rhythm of Leadership

"Is the rhythm of leadership jumping from success to success?" asked an inquisitive friend.

"I wish it was, but not for me," I answered. "The real rhythm of leadership is trial and error, tuning and testing," I said. "To reach our goals, we learn to test, tune, and trust our calling. How we recover from failure shapes the essence of our leadership potential."

In our ever-changing, fast-paced world, the tempo of leadership is constantly managing challenges and disruptions. Imagine a red rubber ball that keeps getting kicked. It bounces and rolls. Occasionally, the ball hits an obstacle and ricochets in an unexpected direction. The leader's challenge is to keep the ball springing forward, even when it finds a pothole. Success is a powerful rebound when you hit rock bottom.

The natural rhythm of the seasons teaches sowing and reaping. To bear fruit in the fall, you must plant in the springtime. The harvest is never unexpected. It is a byproduct of a disciplined pattern of sowing the rights things at the rights times. Tests, challenges, conflicts, and uncertainties are certain to come for the leader, and every challenge requires the leader to acclimate to the new environment. Perhaps you are experiencing a season of trials or hardship. Some leaders thrive in adversity, while others dive in adversity, but the call of the leader is everlasting. When we sow seeds of value and service to others, we yield a bountiful harvest.

One leader who persisted through decades of trial and error was Toastmasters International founder Ralph C. Smedley. A quiet, humble man, Smedley graduated from Illinois Wesleyan University in Bloomington, Illinois, in 1903 and became educational director for the Bloomington YMCA. Smedley saw a pressing need for training in public speaking and leadership development. With the Industrial Revolution pulling millions from the countryside to the city, young people looked to the YMCA (and its female counterpart, the YWCA) to provide low-cost housing, wholesome activities, and opportunities for education and development.[74] Smedley felt a calling to empower a new generation of leaders with practical communication and leadership skills vital to professional success.

In the spring of 1905, Smedley organized his first prototype "speaking club" at the Bloomington YMCA; young men received practice in giving short speeches, debating, and meeting etiquette. At weekly meetings, members rotated through various speaking roles, from emcee to speaker, with evaluations provided by the ever-watchful Smedley. The club prospered, but Smedley left Bloomington within a year's time, and the Toastmasters club died shortly thereafter.

In May of 1906, Smedley accepted a position as general secretary of the YMCA in Freeport, Illinois. He carried with him his Toastmasters dream and started a speaking club at the YMCA in the spring of 1907, which rose to fifty members. While in Freeport, Smedley affirmed his belief in the Toastmasters concept. He would later write that "ability in speaking is one of the marks of a leader and training in self-expression through speech is one of the best ways of discovering and developing hidden talents."[75] Smedley left Freeport in 1909, and the Freeport Toastmasters Club closed shortly thereafter.

Smedley then accepted a position as general secretary of the Rock Island, Illinois, YMCA. True to form, Smedley started his signature Toastmasters Club, which rose to seventy-five members. When Smedley left Rock Island, however, the new YMCA director had little interest in continuing Toastmasters, and the club quickly folded.

In September 1919, Smedley left Illinois for opportunities in California. He accepted a position as general secretary at the San Jose YMCA and started a Toastmasters Club, which flourished briefly but died after his departure. In 1922, Smedley moved south to Santa Ana, California, to oversee the building of a new YMCA. The new Santa Ana YMCA was dedicated in the spring of 1924, and by September, Smedley was promoting a new Toastmasters Club. The first meeting on October 24, 1924, was immensely successful, and the club flourished. Smedley seized the moment by forming a leadership structure, electing a temporary chairman and secretary for the nascent club. He then created a "Memorandum of Organization," outlining the purpose, ground rules, and leadership for the new club.[76]

Smedley had struck a nerve in a nation hungry for professional growth opportunities. Soon, Toastmaster clubs began sprouting throughout Southern California. A Toastmasters federation began to take shape in the summer of

1930. By 1933, there were eighteen clubs, including chapters in Berkeley, California; Seattle, Washington; Tucson, Arizona; and Victoria, British Colombia.

Toastmasters International never would have happened without the entrepreneurial vision of its persistent founder. Smedley pursued his calling by establishing a success rhythm: Wherever he went, he started a speaking club. If it failed, he started another one. Each failure positioned him to learn and grow. Critics saw Smedley's speaking clubs as a passing fad. Smedley saw his speaking clubs as a way to change the world one person at a time.

Leadership is a jagged edge, not a straight line, heaving us through trials, disappointments, and even seasons of failure and despair. Hard surfaces can make the rebound stronger and faster. When things go bad, leadership resolve is tested. Trials can paralyze the leader with feelings of inadequacy and fear. How do you react? Do you become sullen and withdrawn or vocal with anger? Do you assign blame instead of generating solutions?

Leaders develop elastic resilience through positive planning and visualization. What happens to the leader is not nearly as important as how they react to what happens to them. A stable rhythm gives the leader an elastic spirit that helps them bounce back from adversity. Strong leaders make a habit of failing forward. They leave margin for the twists and turns. The faster you fail, the faster you can learn resiliency—a valued trait for the leader. When confronted with failure, leaders resist the temptation to blame others or play the victim. They know failure is not the opposite of success; rather, it is a stepping stone to success.

Failure teaches aspiring leaders to be nimble and flexible. The most successful entrepreneurs often succeed in businesses quite different from the ones they intended.

Henry Wells and partners founded American Express in 1850 as an express mail service—long before it emerged as a worldwide financial services powerhouse. McDonald's founder Ray Kroc sold malted milk machines before he sold hamburgers. Versatile leaders try one pathway until a more promising opportunity emerges.

The rhythm of trial and error is valuable only if we learn from our failures. Failure is both the leader's biggest fear and biggest learning opportunity. While nobody strives to fail, failing early and often creates a resilient, adaptive spirit crucial to success. As a trial attorney, I have learned much more from the cases I have lost. When the witness withers, the facts crumble, or the jury slumbers, I have learned to adapt and cope.

As leaders innovate and take risks, the rhythm of success and failure is something to be expected, not condemned. Failure causes the leader to revise and change course or die. The byproduct of fixing failure is an adaptive organization. The worst failure is having no reason to innovate and becoming enamored with current processes that quickly become obsolete.

The Rhythm of Replenishment

My home is blocks from a quiet California beach. Experiencing the waves washing upon the shoreline is both relaxing and energizing. The waves come in and out with a regular rhythm, varying in size and impact. Like the challenges of leadership, no two waves are exactly the same. Effective leaders establish a rhythm of work and rest, like the ebb and flow of the waves. Imagine if the waves were constantly flowing out—we would have worldwide flooding. On the other hand, imagine if the waves were constantly ebbing—

the oceans would run dry. The rhythm of the flow and ebb balances work and rest for the leader.

Leadership done well is hard work, and maintaining peak performance requires regular replenishment. When you are living in sync with your rhythm, there are times to center your life with playfulness, rest, and fun. What is your centering activity? For me, it is exercise and meditation. When I take my dog for a long walk on the shoreline, it does wonders for my soul.

Great music is enriched by the periods of rest. So are great leaders. *"Rest and self-care are so important. When you take time to replenish your spirit, it allows you to serve from the overflow. You cannot serve from an empty vessel,"* said Eleanor Brownn.[77] Sadly, many leaders confuse selfishness with self-care. Selfishness is taking more than you need; self-care is taking all that you need.

I learned the importance of self-care while campaigning for Toastmasters International office. At the time, I was in my late forties but found myself getting tired in the early afternoon. Candidates require energy and enthusiasm around the clock. A walking zombie does no good. My physical limits were preventing me from conducting a vibrant campaign. I adopted an exercise, diet, and rest program. I stayed away from alcohol, tobacco, and drugs to relieve anxiety. I swam early in the morning, did yoga, and stopped working after dinner time. I made important personal time for my pet, friends, and family. Slowly, my stamina increased, my mental clarity improved, and I was generally happier and more engaged.

Leaders who lack physical, mental, and emotional health have little to offer others. Everyone suffers when a leader's health declines. Many leaders struggle with doing too much, always striving to complete another project. They push to the edge of their abilities, exhausting themselves and those around them. Such leaders end up disdaining the calling they once loved. I have seen leaders collapse, lose control, or suffer a stroke or heart attack.

Watch for danger signs with the people you lead. Often, the best leaders are the ones most susceptible to self-neglect and burnout. When I served as Toastmasters district leader, I had one division governor who was the hardest working, most productive Toastmaster in the district. He trained all his officers, visited all his clubs, and was exemplary in everything he did. One day he disappeared and stopped returning my calls. I discovered his wife had left him and his marriage was on the rocks. I insisted he step back from Toastmasters responsibilities and work on his marriage. Today, he is happily married and has returned to serve as an effective district leader.

Leadership is filled with interruptions. Life interrupts with a dying parent, rebellious teenager, or suffering spouse. Suddenly, the best-laid plans go out the window. The concept of work/life balance is a common aspiration—but not a reality. While I write this chapter, the current international president of Toastmasters from Australia, Mike Storkey, is having unexpected foot surgery. He requested that I fill in for him at a district conference where he was scheduled to speak in Provo, Utah, with only a week's notice. Of course, I found a way to say yes. Spending a long weekend with Toastmaster friends is part of the ebb and flow of my life rhythm.

Summary

Rhythm is the heartbeat of leadership, and it plays strongest when nobody realizes it is playing. Optimize your leadership rhythm by strategically lifting the mood of your organization. Affirm activities that inspire and bring others together. The leader's brand resonates with a cadence that inspires others to say yes together. By saying yes, team members learn to dream, believe, and strive in a positive future together. Conversely, if you squander rhythm, watch the communal culture fall into the valley of despair.

Changing the rhythm is the hardest work of the leader. By setting the example, leaders become the human thermostat that inspires excellence by comforting the afflicted and afflicting the comforted. Leaders are not afraid to push the reset button when negative energy drowns an organization. Leaders know that actions, much more than words, shape the culture and success of teams.

Leaders find the winning rhythm by playing the high notes of attitude, aptitude, and altitude. They are sensitive to others, calling out the high notes to keep others looking up, playing up, and living up to positive expectations. They make use of consistent communications to build relationships and inspire teamwork.

The rhythm of leadership is trial and error. Those unwilling to fail will never experience real success. Make every setback a setup for future success. Make every adversity an opportunity to build personal resilience. Live in sync with your life rhythm to maximize personal energy, like the ebb and flow of the waves. Find a centering activity and make it part of your life.

Timing for the leader is never an accident. Successful leaders set a winning tempo by engaging others to follow, grow, and achieve. For many years, I lived in an apartment above a practicing musician. I heard more rehearsals than a mouse at Carnegie Hall. Mealtime included humming the latest practice tune wafting through my floorboard. Soon, I felt the cadence organizing my thoughts and actions. I began to anticipate the cadence of the music. When the musician finally moved away, I missed his regular musical interludes and felt something was missing. The rhythm of a true leader continues long after the music stops.

8 LEGACY

W ho is the most influential leader in your life? Is it a famous politician, entrepreneur, or entertainer? Probably not. For most of us, the most influential leader is someone who touches us personally—a caring parent, an interested teacher, or a passionate coach. These special people leave an enduring legacy that transcends words. "Carve your name on hearts, not tombstones. A legacy is etched into the minds of others and the stories they share about you," said Shannon L. Alder.[78] *In fact, a legacy is more about who you are than what you say. If you live your life valuing others and building value in them, your actions will speak louder than words.*

If you act on your call to leadership and follow the instructions of this book, you will become the strong leader you are meant to be. At times, you may sizzle or fizzle, and others may cheer you or jeer you—but you will finish knowing that you followed your truest, best course. The formula is simple: Discover your calling, feel your calling, and follow your calling. Personal calling is the compass that guides leadership fulfillment and success.

While a leader's calling begins as something personal, it often finishes as something public. The inner voice that once called you to create, build, and produce will signal a time to release your life's work. While a calling engages and energizes, it also releases you to let go. Your leadership work should finish as authentically as it started.

Legacy leaders leave the world a better place for people they never meet. None of us last forever, although many leaders act like they do! The final transition is often the greatest challenge. For the leader—once the center of attention—departure can bring forlorn thoughts of no longer being needed. Some leaders resist it; others embrace it; still others deny it or even sabotage it and die in their work. Some pretend to retire only to return at the first sight of problems.

Are you ready to transition to a new generation of leaders? Imagine competing as a runner in the 4 X 100 meter relay in the finals of the summer Olympics. Your goal is to skillfully pass the baton in full stride to the next runner without losing speed. A careless stumble or hesitation loses the race for everyone. Every runner stays in stride during the crucial transition period. Leaders must approach transitions with the same attention, care, and coordination. It's not enough to be an effective leader in your time; great leadership passes excellence forward for a new generation.

Leaders Are Stewards

Leadership transition is boosted through revisiting a thought from the opening chapter of this book: Leadership is stewardship. Quite simply, stewardship is service that cares for the property of another. As leaders, we are stewards of our dreams, stewards of our common resources, and stewards of the good we create in the world. Leaders with a stewardship mindset serve others, knowing they are accountable to a larger purpose, a higher calling.

I learned stewardship through a summer caretaker job. As a teenager, I served as the summer custodian for a luxury mansion in my hometown southwest of Chicago. It was our local Palace of Versailles. The wealthy owners spent summers in the south of France and needed someone to watch their prized property. I spent summers cutting the grass, weeding the garden, feeding the pets, and securing the property from intruders. Often, visitors knocked on the front door, asking for a donation or a favor of some kind. I enjoyed the feeling of importance—visitors assumed I was the rich guy who owned the place! I maintained and protected the property as if it were my own, and I enjoyed the relief of returning the keys to the owner at the end of the summer, knowing I was leaving the home better than I had found it.

As leaders, we are stewards of the organizations we guide, direct, and build. Will we leave them in improved condition? Will we protect them from intruders? The future belongs to those who carry our vision forward. The success of new leaders is our success, and their failure is our failure. Imagine you are charged with caring for a beautiful new Rolls Royce. Would you give the keys to your crazy, cracked cousin who drinks and drives? I hope not. Finding future leaders is critical to fulfilling your leadership calling.

Renowned financial educator Dave Ramsey has made legacy planning a top priority in his organization. With a staff of over 500 employees based in Brentwood, Tennessee, he realized that much of his success was based on his personal brand, with content distributed in books, radio, television, and conferences. Ramsey realized the day was coming when his organization would need to run without him.

Ramsey began by inculcating his own children with the bedrock principle of his financial teaching: No debt, no debt, and no debt. Ramsey has put his children through ten years of intense training to prepare them for leadership responsibilities. He has also prepared non-Ramsey family members for leadership by allowing them to speak at his seminars and supporting their book sales. Ramsey is so meticulous he even tracks non-Dave-Ramsey revenue to ensure independent sources of revenue keep growing. Of course, Ramsey practices what he preaches by avoiding all debt, so his organization has the reserves to weather difficult times.

Ramsey embodies a stewardship approach to leadership. He knows leadership is a commitment to a process bigger than himself, and he is quick to support the emerging brand personalities within his organization. He says, "I'm using my platform to launch their brands from so they get a head start. The goal would be that the revenue produced by that group eclipses mine, which is an indication of the survivability of this organization upon succession."[79]

A leader gradually diminishes in importance but not significance. Lao Tzu said it best: "A leader is best when people barely know that he exists, not so good when people obey and acclaim him, worst when they despise him. Fail to honor people, they fail to honor you. But of a good leader, who talks little, when his work is done, his aims fulfilled, they will all say, 'We did this ourselves.'"[80] The power of building an enduring legacy is working yourself out of a job.

Preparing for Succession

Preparing for future leadership helps ensure there will be a future. Each generation raises new leaders to carry the work forward. The leader's time, talent, and energy can make a positive impact in shaping the future, or it can be wasted. I have found there are four keys to successful leadership succession: pause, plan, position, and pass.

- **Pause**: Reflect on the humanity of your leadership work. The frenetic pace of work often distracts us from recognizing our deeper impact. What difference have you made? How are lives transformed by your leadership? Has your calling been fulfilled or barely started? Are you transitioning too early or too late? Are others better suited to meet emerging opportunities and threats because of you? The pause that refreshes will help you recognize the essential value to carry forward.

- **Plan**: Succession planning develops the human capital necessary to carry leadership forward. The key to legacy planning is who, where, how, what, and when. Who are the people best suited for leadership? Where will they come from? How will you train, mentor, and coach potential leaders? What are the weaknesses and threats to the organization that must be addressed by future leaders? A good plan aligns human capital to achieve organizational goals.

- **Position**: Begin positioning future leaders for success. The best way to vet an emerging leader is to give them a position or title. New leaders gain the confidence of knowing that others have confidence in them. Each position provides a platform to flourish or fail, succeed or stumble. But remember: "It's not the position that ultimately makes the leader; it is the leader that makes the position," states John C. Maxwell.[81] A promotion provides an opportunity for greater influence and responsibility, but the new leader needs to make the best of that opportunity.

- **Pass**: All leaders face a time when they must pass the reigns of leadership to others. The process of transitioning to new leadership can happen gradually or quickly, formally or informally. Letting go of authority can be a heart-wrenching, scary process for the leader. But the investment you make in building the next generation of leaders will ease the transition. When new leaders have the proven skill, knowledge, and insight to succeed, the exiting leader has the joy of knowing the future is bright.

Succession planning requires readiness to change leadership at any moment. How would your organization fare if all your top leaders left tomorrow? Would your organization survive? Many leaders only realize the importance of succession planning when it is too late. Implementing a succession plan is a great way to boost team morale. As teams think together about an envisioned future, they create energy and they care for the collective work. Succession planning has a special appeal to the millennial generation (ages eighteen to thirty-five), who are now the largest share of the American workforce. They want to feel valued, appreciated, and part of the organization's success. They want opportunities for quick advancement and engagement.

Making leadership succession a priority pays big dividends for your organization. When you invest in future leaders, providing opportunities for more challenging work, team members feel appreciated. They become faithful, motivated, and dedicated to your organization.

You strengthen company culture and teach important values and skills necessary for success.

Barriers to Leadership Transition

Leadership change is difficult. When the current leadership is well-known and established, the process is even more challenging. Often, the obstacles to leadership transition can seem insurmountable. Fear of change causes many to resist leadership transition at all costs. Openly facing the obstacles to leadership transition is crucial. These common obstacles hold organizations back from embracing a positive, hopeful future:

- **Lack of Humility**: Some popular leaders become cult personalities, boasting organizations that are lengthened shadows of themselves. "I am irreplaceable," they insist. "The organization could never survive without me!" These big-ego leaders perceive any replacement leader as a threat. Why release control to someone who might do better? These leaders are part of the problem, not the solution. They work to doom, rather than groom future leaders. When the elephants fight, the grass gets trampled. Aspiring young leaders feel the discord and leave for better opportunities.

- **Lack of Time**: Leaders are busy people, pressured to do more with less. An overloaded schedule may leave little time for leadership training. The tyranny of the urgent often displaces the valuable leadership development opportunities. Effective leaders make time work for them. They prioritize and delegate everything possible. They duel-track leadership development by training new leaders in the midst of ongoing challenges.

- **Lack of Candidates**: The lack of qualified leadership candidates limits organizational growth. Leaders find a way to recruit quality candidates, knowing future leaders will never emerge from a weak candidate pool. Legacy-minded leaders nurture a supportive culture, which attracts and promotes high-producing leaders.

- **Lack of Confidence**: Some leaders lack confidence in their ability to train and develop new leaders. Think of the talented star athlete who walks on the field and shines but cannot help others do the same. Leadership development is a team effort. It requires more than just human resources input and may reveal organizational weaknesses that require immediate attention.

- **Lack of Accountability**: Leaders foster a culture of ownership and collective investment in the future. Team members are engaged and responsible. This culture extends to training and developing emerging leaders. Leaders know they are ultimately accountable for developing future leaders, and establish benchmarks for leadership development.

Many organizations lack leadership depth; they are just one major accident away from chaos. Ask the average leaders "What are you doing to personally develop future leaders?" and you will receive mixed responses. Sadly, busy leaders do not do enough to prepare for the inevitable. Building a robust transition plan requires facing and conquering these barriers to leadership transition.

Called leaders invest in the future. They slowly work themselves out of a job by cultivating talent wherever they find it. In the investment world, money can grow incrementally through the passage of time. Small, systematic contributions over a decade can yield a bountiful treasure.

Similarly, future leaders grow through systematic support, training, and encouragement. Making the time to coach, mentor, and encourage others develops the human capital necessary for strong future leaders.

Every organization craves successful leaders, but few do the work necessary to develop them. Successful leaders make time to develop their replacement. They confront the obstacles to leadership development by investing in people. People are the most valuable asset of any organization. Technology, real estate, and buildings can all be duplicated or copied by your competition. But your people are unique; they define your organizational culture and can never be duplicated.

C-Level Leadership Qualities

Leadership development and transition should be intentional, not accidental. To find future leaders, spend time identifying high-potential candidates. Without an intentional approach, you may find yourself settling for the best-available candidate when time is short.

C-level leaders are the highest ranking executives in any organization. The letter C stands for chief. While the title is intimidating, C-level leaders can make or break your organization. The selection process takes time, and it should not be rushed. Develop a pool of potential replacement leaders who share the vision and values of the organization. They should possess complementary skills and attributes to take the organization to the next level. Be open to a leader who breaks with the past or wants to pursue new opportunities. Look for the leader who grows the vision and builds cohesion within diversity. Never settle for sizzle over substance. The right leader is waiting to be discovered.

What qualities should you look for in future leaders? While every leadership opportunity is unique, testing for C-level qualities requires a sense of calling, character, and competency:

- **Calling**: Look for aspiring leaders with a sense of personal calling. Work is more than a perfunctory task; it is an inspiring journey, filled with discovery, intrigue, and personal growth. The word for occupational work—vocation—is derived from the Latin word vocare, which means to call. Called leaders are not afraid to stretch or sacrifice to achieve desired goals. They adopt an open mindset, learning from every adversity. Helping others become aware of their calling is crucial to long-term success and should be a regular part of every leadership development program.

- **Character**: "Character is doing what is right when nobody is looking," said former US speaker of the house J. C. Watts.[82] Leaders who are honest and forthright engender trust in others. They avoid office politics and show genuine concern for others. Character is built day by day, month my month, and year by year by ethical decisions. Leaders who speak the truth and live the truth grow a strong and robust character.

- **Competency**: Competency is the acquired acumen to do and say what needs to be done. It does not mean you know all the answers, but you *do* know where to get the best-quality information. Competent leaders demonstrate high-level communication skills. They know how to bring people together through inclusive language. As confidence in the leader grows, the social bonds that link team members grow to maximize performance. Each human endeavor has a different measurement for competency, and the bar of excellence is always being adjusted. Growing leaders are constantly studying and working to do their jobs better, building competencies in communication, problem solving, emotional intelligence, and other important fields.

Nurturing C-level qualities is a lifelong process. More is caught than taught. If you demonstrate C-level qualities in your own life, you will attract those who want to be like you. It reminds me of a story of Alexander the Great, one of the greatest military leaders of all time. By the age of thirty-three, he had conquered most of the known world. In fall of 325, he led his troops on a march across the Gedrosian desert (part of modern-day Iran). The summer sun scorched the troops, and there was no water. After 75 kilometers and eleven days in the desert, the troops were dying in droves from thirst and heat exhaustion. [83] One especially hot day, two scouts summoned by Alexander brought him a most prized possession: a cup of water.

He lifted the cup high and poured it into the searing sand. "Not one shall drink while many thirst," he said. In that moment, Alexander publically affirmed his calling, his character, and his competence as a leader. His bold sacrifice became a source of inspiration, attracting C-level leaders to rise in triumph. His actions spoke louder than words. The seemingly small act made a big statement. Spurred by the devotion of their leader, the troops persisted through the desert to complete a successful campaign.

I am grateful for the mentors who challenged me to persist through the desert and grow C-level qualities. Grooming future leaders is a job that never ceases. Smart organizations view leadership development as an ongoing process, not a solitary training event. High-talent leaders are identified early in their career, provided challenging growth opportunities, and afforded the best feedback, training, and coaching available. Leaders become a fountain of inspiration, providing what is most needed, wanted, and expected to succeed.

Leadership Diamonds

Finding leaders is like mining for diamonds. Leaders emerge from unsuspecting places when least expected. It reminds me of a favorite story: A South African man spent his life cultivating an arid almond farm south of Johannesburg. The work was grueling and exhausting. He farmed the dry, arid land from sunrise to sunset, just as his father and father's father had done. His return was the pittance of a meager harvest each year. The farmer rarely made a subsistence wage and often borrowed money just to survive.

As the decades rolled by, the farmer became frustrated, disillusioned, and discouraged. He longed for a better life. He yearned for prosperity, wealth, and success. So he packed his bags for good and abandoned the old farm in the sunset of life. He moved to the big city of Johannesburg, hoping for a better opportunity. The best job he could find was as a bookkeeper, making less than he had made farming. He died a poor man.

After his death, a government surveyor was mapping the old farm one day and noticed a gleaming crystal resting at the bottom of a dry streambed. The surveyor became curious and took a closer look. It was a diamond! Additional investigation revealed the old farm was one of the largest depositories of natural diamonds in the world. The farmer had wasted his life in poverty while standing on his own acres of diamonds.

This popular "Acres of Diamonds" story originates from a nineteenth century preacher and Civil War deserter named

Russell Conwell. Variations on the story have been told and adapted for decades. Conwell retold the story hundreds of times to successfully raise funds to found Temple University in Philadelphia, Pennsylvania. He believed all of us have unused, undiscovered potential within—right at our own feet. Conwell challenged dreamers to search for riches close to home. While the grass always seems greener someplace else, our own grass can look as good (or better!) with proper care and feeding. Our true potential lies in looking at what we already have—discovering the rich resources that lie at our feet and developing them. Every company mining precious metals has a process for identifying and extracting the diamonds. What is yours?

Leaders find buried treasure in unlikely places. They see people not as they are but as they can be. They recognize the untapped potential in themselves and others, and create a process for developing human capital. "When we treat a man as he is, we make him worse than he appears. When we treat him as if he already was what he potentially could be, we make him what he should be," wrote von Goethe.[84] Knowing greatness lies within, leaders are constantly on the hunt for people with talent.

The unpolished stone that becomes a leadership diamond may pass through many hands before it is revealed. Leadership succession planning requires finding diamonds in the rough. Through coaching, mentoring, and support, the rough spots are polished and leadership talent is revealed. Leaders flourish *internally* before they flourish *externally*. The strong character and consistency necessary to be an effective leader is established early, then built through developmental experiences.

Contrary to popular opinion, there is no shortage of ambitious leaders. Hartford's 2015 Leadership Survey found that 69 percent of millennials aspire to be leaders in the next five years.[85] The leadership challenge is recognizing and cultivating the people of influence. A called leader is engaged and passionate, caring about what they do and how they do it. They display unfaltering energy to be more, go further, and do better. They are self-aware, resilient to adversity, and capable of flexible thinking. Their potential is demonstrated in small achievements, which reveal their calling, character, and competency.

The Rewards of Leadership

Leadership rewards flow to those who lean into their vision, discover their talents, and serve others. Called leaders build a platform for influence, releasing potential and power in others. The work always takes longer than planned. The challenges are more than anticipated.

On the surface, the rewards of leadership appear elusive. Leadership may leave us feeling tired and irritable, pulled by ever increasing stress and pressure. At times, we may feel anxious and disappointed. If you stay true to your calling and persist, however, positive rewards appear like a rainbow after the rain.

The REWARDS of leadership come in seven distinct areas:

- **R**elationships: Leaders establish and maintain strong, trusted relationships. The human touch unifies the leadership team. Team members are happy to work for a leader who cares about them. Genuine leaders know that people are not the means to an end; people are the end. As leaders invest in others, they build successful relationships, which become their enduring legacy.

- Excellence: Leaders build a culture that values, promotes, and produces excellence. When we examine our attitudes, we uncover self-limiting thoughts and beliefs. When we examine our habits, we confront poor practices that can be improved. Leaders raise the bar, expecting more from themselves and others, and building a culture of continuous improvement.

- Wealth: Leadership is the most sought-after skill in the world, and organizations will pay handsomely for skilled leaders. While there are plenty of competent managers, leaders are rare. Though a stout bank account is not the main reason to lead, it is certainly a welcome result. Of course, all success is relative. The more success you have, the more relatives you have!

- Ability: Leadership will help you develop abilities you did not know you possessed. Leadership stretches you to become more and develop everything you have to serve others. If you never lead, you never recognize the full scope of your potential.

- Respect: Respect is earned when leaders consistently deliver value. They do the right thing and absorb the consequences. Words alone do not create respect. Actions speak louder than words. When a leader's positive behaviors reinforce their words, respect is born. When it continues over a lifetime, respect becomes engrained.

- Depth: The deepest and most lasting reward of leadership is personal growth. Leadership brings us face-to-face with our inner inadequacies and weaknesses. Until we surrender to the potential within, we never experience the full depths of possibility. We dig deeply into our human resources and emerge deeply grounded and aware. The impact of leadership is deep, wide, and strong in making us more valuable and resourceful to our society.

- Service: "True leadership must be for the benefit of the followers, not the enrichment of the leaders," said Robert Townsend.[86] Leaders enjoy the satisfaction of investing in the lives of others. Their stewardship enriches the lives of others. Leaders who serve others well enjoy a lasting legacy of appreciation.

The rewards of leadership reflect the abundance of what we create in the world. Quality leadership improves the collective quality of life for everyone. Some of the best rewards flow from our rich life experience. We go places we never dreamed of going and meet people we never dreamed of meeting. The pride of handing off leadership successfully to others enhances our self-worth and personal respect. When we sustain quality, we enjoy a fulfilling legacy.

Often, the distractions and temptations of life pull us away from our true calling. We sacrifice the great for the good. We opt for the comfortable and convenient, instead of the exciting and challenging. You know you are missing the mark when your work brings constant frustration and burnout. In contrast, hitting the sweet spot of your calling brings joy, power, and achievement. You do things few can match.

Accepting the call of the leader generates confidence— the assurance of doing the right things in the right way—and the rewards are commensurate with the task undertaken. Each of us makes an individual decision to answer the call or ignore it. Called leadership culminates in a challenging and rewarding life.

Last Call

The last call is rarely a surprise. While this book is coming to an end, your authentic leadership journey is just beginning. Our world is calling out for reliable, capable leaders. Although the challenges are great, the rewards are rich and bountiful. Will you answer the call? World problems like disease, poverty, hunger, war, illiteracy, and climate change are waiting for a creative, proactive leader to rise up. Nothing happens until a leader feels the need, hears the call, and takes action.

There is a quiet, still voice that moves your spirit. While reading this book, have you heard the hopeful calling, the hard calling, the hidden calling, or the higher calling? More than shallow reflection, the call of the leader aligns the hole in your soul with the hope of our world. The inner voice beckons you in the highs and lows of life and everyplace in between. Will you seize the opportunity to test, tune, and trust your calling?

My leadership journey has brought fulfillment through service. Since answering the call to leadership as Toastmasters International president in 2011–2012, my life has paid handsome dividends, and I have never looked back. My law firm has grown. My speaking audiences have grown. My influence has grown. Most importantly, I have played a role in launching a new generation of leaders eager to grow, serve, and achieve.

As a boy growing up west of Chicago, my favorite pastime was going to the park. The park was a wonderland of opportunity. There were ball games, scavenger hunts, and hide-and-seek games. But the best part of going to the park was buying a helium balloon.

When the weather was good, a helium balloon salesman showed up on Saturday mornings at the park with a helium tank and a few packages of colorful balloons. He sold red balloons, green balloons, orange balloons, blue balloons, purple balloons, yellow balloons, and violet balloons. If sales got a little slow, the salesman would release a balloon into the air. Children would notice the balloon rising on the landscape and rally around the salesman to buy more balloons. By the end of the day, the salesman ran out of the most popular colors.

Late one day, the balloon salesman gave a last call for balloons. A little boy approached the salesmen with tears in his eyes. "You don't have the color I want," he sobbed. "What good is a balloon with the wrong color?"

"Don't worry, son," said the balloon salesman. "It is not what is on the outside that makes a balloon rise; it is what is on the inside."

ENDNOTES

1. Global Workforce Leadership Survey (2015). https://workplacetrends.com/the-global-workforce-leadership-survey/.

2. Ibid.

3. National Leadership Index 2012: A National Study of Confidence in Leadership, Center for Public Leadership (2012). Cambridge, Massachusetts: Harvard Kennedy School, Harvard University. http://andresraya.com/wp-content/uploads/2012/12/cpl_nli_2012.pdf.

4. Riddle, Douglas (2016). "Executive Integration: Equipping Transitioning Leaders for Success." Center for Creative Leadership (website). https://www.ccl.org/wp-content/uploads/2015/04/ExecutiveIntegration.pdf.

5. Merriam-Webster Online Dictionary. https://www.merriam-webster.com/dictionary/calling.

6. "Forbes 400 Richest Americans" (2013). Forbes (website). http://www.forbes.com/special-report/2013/forbes-400/ones-to-watch/david-copperfield.html.

7. Parr, Jerry, and Carolyn Parr (2013). In the Secret Service: The True Story of the Man who Saved President Reagan's Life. Illinois: Tyndale House Publishers.

8. Stack, Liam (October 10, 2015). "Jerry Parr, Secret Service Agent Who Helped Save Reagan, Dies at 85." New York Times.

9. Ibid.

10. Swindoll, Charles (2009). Paul: A Man of Grace and Grit. Nashville, Tennessee: Thomas Nelson Publishers.

11. "Top Leader Quotes: Conrad Hilton." Top Leader VT (website). http://topleadervt.com/top-leader-quotes-conrad-hilton/.

12. King, Martin Luther Jr. (1999). "Voices on Resistance, Renewal and Reform" in Let Nobody Turn Us Around: An African American Anthology. Rowman and Littlefield Publishers.

13. Frost, Robert. Brainy Quote. https://www.brainyquote.com/quotes/quotes/r/robertfros151833.html.

14. Tzu, Lao. Brainy Quote. https://www.brainyquote.com/quotes/lao_tzu_379183.

15. Allen, Robert (2009). The One Minute Millionaire: The Enlightened Way to Wealth. New York City, New York: Three Rivers Press.

16. Merriam-Webster Online Dictionary. https://www.merriam-webster.com/dictionary/passion.

17. Online Etymology Dictionary. http://www.etymonline. com/index.php?term=vitality.

18. Online Etymology Dictionary http://www.etymonline. com/index.php?term=inspiration.

19. "Charles Schwab: Budget Broker." Entrepreneur Magazine (online). https://www.entrepreneur.com/ article/197694.

20. https://www.entrepreneur.com/article/197694

21. "The Cavett Award." National Speakers Association (website). https://www.nsaspeaker.org/cavett-award/.

22. Robert, Cavett (1969). Success with People. The Napoleon Hill Foundation.

23. Kan, Michelle, Allen Li, et al. "Job Satisfaction: 2016 Edition: Tightening Labor Market Means More Opportunity, More Satisfaction." The Conference Board (website). https://www.conference-board.org/publications/ publicationdetail.cfm?publicationid=7250&centerId=4.

24. Holmes, Oliver W. Goodreads Quotes. http://www. goodreads.com/quotes/222999-many-people-die-with-their-music-still-in-them-too.

25. Kriegel, Robert and Louis Patler (1991). If it Ain't Broke ... Break It! And Other Unconventional Wisdom for a Changing World. Little, Brown and Company.

26. Craig, Nick and Scott A. Snook. "From Purpose to Impact." Harvard Business Review (May 2014 issue). https://hbr.org/2014/05/from-purpose-to-impact.

27. Rohn, Jim. Brainy Quote. https://www.brainyquote.com/ quotes/jim_rohn_133000.

28. Shakespeare, William. Twelfth Night (Act II, Scene V). http://www.bartleby.com/70/2325.html.

29. "Massachusetts Bay: The City Upon a Hill." U.S. History Online Textbook. http://www.ushistory.org/us/3c.asp.

30. "Vision, Mission Statement, and Objective." What Is Human Resources (website). http://www.whatishumanresource.com/vision-mission-and-goals.

31. Berra, Yogi (2002). *When You Come to a Fork in the Road, Take It!: Inspiration and Wisdom from One of Baseball's Greatest Heroes.* New York: Hyperion.

32. Buchan, John (1930). Montrose and Leadership. London: Oxford University Press.

33. "Who We Are." Toastmasters International (website). https://www.toastmasters.org/about/who-we-are.

34. Benson, Mary (1986). Nelson Mandela. Harmondsworth: Penguin Books.

35. Meredith, Martin (2010). *Mandela: A Biography.* New York: PublicAffairs.

36. Thoreau, Henry David (1854). Walden. Boston: Ticknor and Fields.

37. Hugo, Victor (1877). Histoire d'un Crime (The History of a Crime).

38. Williams, Arthur. AZ Quotes. http://www.azquotes.com/author/36622-Arthur_L_Williams_Jr.

39. Hill, Napoleon. Brainy Quote. https://www.brainyquote.com/quotes/napoleon_hill_392258.

40. Walker, Alice. Wikiquote (website). https://en.wikiquote.org/wiki/Alice_Walker.

41. Merriam-Webster Online Dictionary. https://www.merriam-webster.com/dictionary/charisma.

42. Hobbes, Thomas (1909–1914). Of Man, Being the First Part of Leviathan. The Harvard Classics. http://www.bartleby.com/34/5/10.html.

43. Creative Commons. A Primer on Communications Studies. http://2012books.lardbucket.org/books/a-primer-on-communication-studies/s04-nonverbal-communication.html.

44. Carnegie, Dale (1956). How to Develop Self-Confidence and Influence by Public Speaking. Simon and Schuster.

45. King, Martin Luther Jr. (2010). Strength to Love. Minneapolis: Fortress Press.

46. Nin, Anaïs (1969). Diary of Anaïs Nin, Volume 3, 1939–1944. San Diego, California: Harcourt Brace Jovanovich.

47. Peck, M. Scott (1978). The Road Less Traveled. New York: Random House.

48. Silverstein, Richard (March 22, 2004). "Jewish Humor: Want to Win the Lottery? Buy a ticket!" Tikun Olam (website). https://www.richardsilverstein.com/2004/03/22/jewish-humor-wa/.

49. https://www.etymonline.com/word/conviction.

50. Allen, Robert (2009). The One Minute Millionaire: The Enlightened Way to Wealth. New York City, New York: Three Rivers Press.

51. Gide, André (1925). Les faux-monnayeurs [The Counterfeiters] in Nouvelle Revue Française.

52. https://www.bbc.com/timelines/zqp7tyc

53. Martin, L., J. Davison, O. Orasanu, et al. "Identifying error-inducing contexts in aviation." Paper presented at SAE World Aviation Conference (October 19–21,

1999) in San Francisco, CA. https://www.sae.org/publications/technical-papers/content/1999-01-5540/.

54. As quoted in Boxer's Bible of Counterpunching: The Killer Response to Any Attack by Mark Hatmaker (2012).

55. https://www.finebooksmagazine.com/fine_books_blog/2009/02/sullys-lost-book.phtml

56. https://web.archive.org/web/20090208151435/http://accessinterviews.com:80/interviews/detail/chesley-b-sullenberger-iii/12009

57. Cabot, Meg. Goodreads Quotes. http://www.goodreads.com/quotes/317879-the-brave-may-not-live-forever-but-the-cautious-do.

58. Mehrabian, A. (1972). Nonverbal communication. Aldine-Atherton, Chicago, Illinois.

59. Burning Glass Technologies (2015). "The Human Factor." Burning Glass (website). http://burning-glass.com/wp-content/uploads/Human_Factor_Baseline_Skills_FINAL.pdf.

60. King, Martin Luther Jr. (September 1, 1958). "My Pilgrimage to Nonviolence." The Martin Luther King Jr. Research and Education Institute. https://kinginstitute.stanford.edu/king-papers/documents/my-pilgrimage-nonviolence.

61. Bryan, William Jennings, ed. (1906). The World's Famous Orations. New York City, New York: Funk & Wagnalls. Introduction available at http://www.bartleby.com/268/.

62. "ForbesQuotes: Thoughts On The Business of Life." Forbes (website). https://www.forbes.com/quotes/7640/.

63. Roosevelt, Franklin D. Brainy Quote. https://www.brainy quote.com/quotes/franklin_d_roosevelt_164074.

64. Zimmer, John. "Quotes for Public Speakers (No. 1)—Mark Twain." Manner of Speaking (blog). https://mannerofspeaking.org/2009/12/07/quotes-for-public-speakers-no-1/.

65. http://www.kokdemir.info/courses/psk301/docs/GibsonWalk_VisualCliff(1960).pdf

66. http://www.dailymail.co.uk/sciencetech/article-2847208/The-sound-STATUS-Powerful-people-develop-loud-high-pitched-monotonous-voices-study-claims.html

67. Morgan, Nick (March 24, 2015). "What's The Right Voice For A Leader?" Forbes (website). https://www.forbes.com/sites/nickmorgan/2015/03/24/whats-the-right-voice-for-a-leader/#5c68b3217596.

68. Branson, Richard. "My Top 10 Quotes on Opportunity." Virgin (website). https://www.virgin.com/richard-branson/my-top-10-quotes-on-opportunity.

69. Hoad, T. F., ed. (February 23, 2007). The Concise Oxford Dictionary of English Etymology. Oxford University Press.

70. Liddel, Henry George and Robert Scott. A Greek English Lexicon. Perseus Digital Library, Tufts University (website).

71. Ziglar, Zig. Brainy Quote. https://www.brainyquote.com/quotes/zig_ziglar_381975.

72. Irving, John. Brainy Quote. https://www.brainyquote.com/quotes/quotes/j/johnirving378460.html.

73. Drexler, Millard. Brainy Quote. https://www.brainyquote.com/quotes/millard_drexler_538202?src=t_consistency.

74. Frost, J. William (1998). "Part V: Christianity and Culture in America" in *Christianity: A Social and Cultural History* (second edition). Upper Saddle River, New Jersey: Prentice Hall.

75. Smedley, Ralph (1993). The Story of Toastmasters. Toastmasters International (publisher). https://www.toastmasters.org/shop/education/books/B1--The-Story-of-Toastmasters.

76. Ibid.

77. Brownn, Eleanor. "Rest and Self-Care ..." Eleanor Brownn (blog). https://eleanorbrownn.wordpress.com/2013/09/04/rest-and-self-care-are-so-important-when-you-take-time-to-replenish-your-spirit-it-allows-you-to-serve-others-from-the-overflow-you-cannot-serve-from-an-empty-vessel/.

78. Alder, Shannon. Pinterest. https://www.pinterest.com/pin/218072806929804527/.

79. Jimenez, Jesus. "Dave Ramsey Has a Plan for the Rest of Your Life." Success Magazine (online). https://www.success.com/article/dave-ramsey-has-a-plan-for-the-rest-of-your-life.

80. Tzu, Lao. Brainy Quote. https://www.brainyquote.com/quotes/authors/l/lao_tzu.html.

81. Economy, Peter. "44 Inspiring John C. Maxwell Quotes for Leadership Success." Inc. Magazine (website). https://www.inc.com/peter-economy/44-inspiring-john-c-maxwell-quotes-that-will-take-you-to-leadership-success.html.

82. Watts, J. C. AZ Quotes. http://www.azquotes.com/author/15365-J_C_Watts.

83. http://www.livius.org/sources/content/arrian/anabasis/alexander-in-the-gedrosian-desert/

84. von Goethe, Johann Wolfgang. Goodreads Quotes. http://www.goodreads.com/quotes/403820-when-we-treat-man-as-he-is-we-make-him.

85. "The Hartford's 2015 Millennial Leadership Survey." https://www.thehartford.com/sites/thehartford/files/millennial-leadership-2015.pdf.

86. Townsend, Robert. QuotationsBook.com. http://quotationsbook.com/quote/22958/.

CPSIA information can be obtained
at www.ICGtesting.com
Printed in the USA
FSHW021444190919
62179FS